Territory

This book introduces readers to the concept of territory as it applies to law while demonstrating the particular work that territory does in organizing property relations.

Territories can be found in all societies and at all scales, although they take different forms. The concern here is on the use of territories in organizing legal relations. Law, as a form of power, often works through a variety of territorial strategies, serving multiple legal functions, such as attempts at creating forms of desired behaviour. Landed property, in Western society, is often highly territorial, reliant on sharply policed borders and spatial exclusion. But rather than thinking of territory as obvious and given or as a natural phenomenon, this book focuses particularly on its relation to property to argue that territory is both a social product and a specific technology that organizes social relations. That is: territory is not simply an outcome of property relations but a strategic means by which such relations are communicated, imagined, legitimized, enforced, naturalized and contested.

Accessible to students, this book will be of interest to those working in the areas of sociolegal studies, geography, urban studies, and politics.

Nicholas Blomley is Professor of Geography at Simon Fraser University, Canada.

Part of the NEW TRAJECTORIES IN LAW
series editors
Adam Gearey, Birkbeck College, University of London
Prabha Kotiswaran, Kings College London
Colin Perrin, Commissioning Editor, Routledge
Mariana Valverde, University of Toronto

For information about the series and details of previous and forthcoming titles, see www.routledge.com/New-Trajectories-in-Law/book-series/NTL

A GlassHouse Book

Territory

New Trajectories in Law

Nicholas Blomley

Routledge
Taylor & Francis Group
a GlassHouse Book

First published 2023
by Routledge
4 Park Square, Milton Park, Abingdon, Oxon OX14 4RN

and by Routledge
605 Third Avenue, New York, NY 10158

Routledge is an imprint of the Taylor & Francis Group, an informa business

A GlassHouse book

British Library Cataloguing-in-Publication Data
A catalogue record for this book is available from the British Library

ISBN: 978-1-032-18200-1 (hbk)
ISBN: 978-1-032-18204-9 (pbk)
ISBN: 978-1-003-25338-9 (ebk)

DOI: 10.4324/9781003253389

Typeset in Bembo
by Apex CoVantage, LLC

I dedicate this book to my teachers.

Contents

Preface

Nicholas Blomley

'So below' (https://sobelow.org) is a graphic essay by cartoonist and journalist Sam Wallman. A powerful critique of the colonial/capitalist landed property system, focused on its 'territorialism and dominion', it critiques private property and the commodification of land while directing us to its spatial manifestation in borders, zones and spaces of exclusion. It opens with a powerfully corporeal statement:

Figure P.1 'We need sum room'.

Source: From sobelow.org; reproduced with permission.

We all need 'sum room'. We are embodied beings who occupy and depend upon space. To have access to 'sum room' is to have some freedom. Put more formally, the liberty to perform an action requires the availability of a space in which one is free to perform that action. 'Everything that is done has to be done somewhere. No one is free to perform an action unless there is somewhere he [she/they] is free to perform it' (Waldron, 1991, p. 296).

One manifestation of space and freedom is a territory, a bounded, contiguous section of the Earth's surface, that is claimed or controlled by a particular group, nation, or state in order to restrict or control spatial access for specific periods. Territory is functional, organized and controlled for particular ends. Territory is very often symbolic, linking the territory to some form of identity. Territory is clearly geographic, entailing the marking out of bounded spaces. It is also temporal, operating at specific times, for example.

Territory, as a topic, has been a longstanding concern within the discipline of Geography, receiving new attention in recent years (see, for example, Elden, 2013; Paasi et al., 2022; Painter, 2010). Reflecting geographer's theorization of space as both a social product and constitutive of social order, territory is understood as social and political rather than as an inert abstract surface or an expression of a transhistorical biological imperative. Territory matters. It is not simply an *outcome* of social relations but a *means* through which such relations are enacted. Rather than an obvious apolitical space, territory can thus be more usefully thought of as 'political technology' (Elden, 2010). Hence we can think of territoriality as the strategic use of territory to achieve certain ends (Sack, 1986). While territories can be observed at multiple scales and put to work to serve multiple ends, geographers tend to consider them as means for thinking about the nation-state. For Dahlman (2009, p. 77), for example, the very definition of territory is 'the spatial extent of the state'. Similarly, for Painter (2010, p. 1090), territory is 'quintessentially state space'.

Sociolegal scholars have given less attention to territory. This is curious, for Western law, in particular, has long relied on a set of territorial understandings regarding law. Medieval European lawyers interpreted Roman law to argue that legal jurisdiction should apply to a bounded space. This marked a crucial shift from the personality of law, which governed members of a defined community, regardless of their location, to the territoriality of law. From this emerged the connections between territory and state sovereignty, echoing the interests of geographers, as noted previously. Law takes place, literally, within the territorial envelope of the state. While, as Benton (2010) notes, the territorial reach of sovereign power has historically been somewhat ambiguous, modern law is committed to a sharply bounded concept of spatial sovereignty.

Because of its roots in state sovereignty, modern law is therefore deeply territorial. Brighenti (2010b) argues that law is centrally concerned with the movement of bodies in space and their control, and thus, law is a 'territorial endeavour, a movement that acts upon other movements' (217). Law, as a form of power, often works through a variety of territorial strategies, serving multiple legal functions. For example, criminal law in Canada controls the spatial movement of people released on bail for petty offences through the extensive use of 'red zones', designed to control behaviour by territorially excluding alleged offenders from designated spaces (Sylvestre et al., 2020).

Yet despite its importance, there is little written on territory and law. Private law, in particular, is rarely thought of through a territorial lens. Take real property, for example. While there are important exceptions, notably the work of Smith (2014), documented later, space has a bad odour for many property scholars. Indeed, one property lawyer characterizes space as a 'forgotten dimension' (Babie, 2013). This reflects the lawyerly truism that property is not a relation between a person and land but a relation between people in regard to land (Hohfeld, 1913). You can't sue an acre. Nor is a boundary dispute a dispute between you and a boundary.

Given the tendency to think of territory through a state-centred lens, geographers interested in territory also don't have a lot to say about property. Perhaps this reflects a desire to avoid the taint of ethology (cf. Ardrey, 1966). Derek Hall's (2013) account of land draws a curious distinction between territory (understood in relation to the national state), regulation (the rules governing the possession and use of land), and property (the right to make decisions relating to land within a structure of regulation), for example. Stuart Elden (2010; see also 2021) does distinguish between the concepts of 'land' (i.e. property) and 'terrain' (i.e. land that has a military, political and strategic value), yet treats the former as a largely political-economic factor.

For this series, I was charged with bringing the concept of territory to bear on law. To do justice to this brief would be beyond the scope of what are intended to be short-form, punchy books. As a result, I have elected to introduce readers to the concept of territory as it applies to real property, filling the gap between property scholarship and geography (and other relevant fields) noted previously. Hopefully, this gives the reader some sense of how territory could be applied to other legal domains. In so doing, I aim to demonstrate the work that territory does in organizing property relations, particularly in relation to land. Our understanding of either property or territory is incomplete, I would argue, without attention to their intersection. In so doing, my hope is to demonstrate the importance of territory to the work of property, particularly in relation to social justice. The need for 'sum room' collides with what Sam Wallman terms our 'territorial tendencies'.

My focus here will be property rules as applied to land. Land is particularly significant in lived social contexts, as it serves diverse, important roles, as noted years ago by a young Winston Churchill:

> Land differs from all other forms of property. . . . Land, which is a necessity of human existence, which is the original source of all wealth, which is strictly limited in extent, which is fixed in geographical position – land, I say, differs from all other forms of property in these primary and fundamental conditions.
>
> (1910/2013, p. 62)

Use of or access to land is crucial for many activities engaged in by humans (and nonhumans), such as agriculture, resource extraction, conservation and, of course, shelter. Land is a rivalrous good – if I grow potatoes in a field, others cannot. Unlike other commodities, land cannot be extracted and removed – it stays still. You can't hide it away or move it like other commodities (Li, 2014).

While we all need 'sum room', the terms under which room is made available are socially differentiated, as Sam Wallman makes clear. Property's territoriality holds some up while confining others to spaces of uncertainty, vulnerability and dispossession. I benefit from the territorial workings of property. Indeed, the protections that propertied space affords me are causally linked with the geographies of precarity (Blomley, 2020a).

The protections of propertied territory were made abundantly clear during the writing of this book, much of which occurred as I 'self-isolated' with covid in England. I did so in my father's house during a rather compromised Christmas visit. The U.K. government required that I isolate myself. Self-isolation, of course, presumes control over space. The property right that my father has ensures

Figure P.2 A quiet, desperate mania.

Source: From sobelow.org; reproduced with permission.

that such control is feasible. For those living without such protections – for example, in a homeless shelter – self-isolation is a dangerously laughable idea. Assuming that people do not have their own self-contained shelter space, the British authorities blithely suggest 'cohorting', or simply gathering people 'into different areas depending on their status'.[1] While we all need 'sum room', as Sam Wallman notes, the realities of propertied territory can quickly generate a 'quiet, desperate mania'.

To summarize what follows, Chapter 1 introduces territory. Territory is not primordial, I argue, but socially produced and productive of social relations. Rather than thinking of territory as obvious and given, or as a natural phenomenon, I will argue that it is both a social product and a particular technology that organizes social relations in distinctive and consequential ways. In other words, territory is not simply an *outcome* of social relations but a *means* by which such relations are enforced, naturalized and contested. Territory has been short-changed in property analysis, I note, appearing obvious or serving only functional purposes. This ignores the lived reality of property. When we encounter property in land, it is likely through its territorial manifestations. Property relations, therefore, are often experienced, judged, enacted, and contested in and through these territorial encounters. Territorializing property relations, moreover, serves to communicate, enforce, legitimize and complicate the relationality of property. In that access to space is a precondition for human flourishing, the particular ways in which property rules are territorialized are a matter of social justice. As such, territory deserves our attention.

Chapter 2 introduces property, pushing back against its dominant characterization (the 'ownership model'), and suggesting that we should view it as inherently relational. Rather than simply a relation between owners and objects, property regulates relations between people. As such, property needs to be understood as a means by which certain forms of social power are allocated, for better or worse. Property rules determine who can, who can't, and who may conditionally use and access resources vital to life and human flourishing, like land. Those who are empowered by property rules have power over other people. Property, therefore, is fundamental to social power, including structures

---

1 www.gov.uk/government/publications/covid-19-guidance-on-services-for-people-experiencing-rough-sleeping/covid-19-guidance-for-commissioners-and-providers-of-hostel-services-for-people-experiencing-homelessness-and-rough-sleeping

such as racism. Property relations, therefore, are power relations. We can think about the ways property structures social relations, I suggest, by noting the ways in which it organizes what I term the 'property space', situating the participants in any property relation, specifying what the participants can do to each other, framing alternatives to transacting, and communicating powerful meanings to the participants.

It is tempting to assume that the property arrangements many of us are familiar with, including their territoriality, have always been with us. However, they are a recent social product. Chapter 3 tracks an important historical moment – early modern rural enclosure in England – when the contemporary hegemonic territorialization of property emerged. As an interaction device, territory helped reconstitute changing property relations, producing new social gradients premised on differential access and use of land. These practices placed increased importance upon a territorial exclusivity that centred on individual rights, most particularly the right of the individual to exclude others from bounded spaces. As such, the legal and practical defence of territory became of more pressing importance. As land became more sharply territorialized, so commoners became deterritorialized. Legal doctrine – notably the very concept of 'property' itself – changed, as did imaginative and practical geographic changes, particularly the practice of land surveying. Powerful new discourses of land management emerged, emphasizing the importance of hedging out the poor. Yet the commoners refused to conform to these new territorial logics, contesting emergent practices of exclusion and challenging the materialized territoriality of enclosure.

Property is produced by and productive of social differences, including racial categories. The evolution of property law has been articulated through the attribution of value to the lives of those defined as having the capacity, will and technology to appropriate, racializing those deemed unfit to own property. The justification for property ownership is thus bound to a highly racialized concept of the human. The social powers that property's territorialization accord are also embedded in such racial logics. Chapter 4 considers the role of territorialized property relations in racialized colonial strategies of dispossession, drawing from the Canadian experience. Colonial settlement, it is argued, entails the simultaneous remaking of property relations and the inauguration of a territorial grid that serves both practically and ideologically to rework social relations to land. Predicated on racialized notions of the human, property's territoriality was, and continues to be, weaponized by settlers. I focus on the installation of a territorialized colonial property system in late nineteenth-century British Columbia and related struggles over access to land between settlers and Indigenous people, drawing from testimony from the McKenna-McBride Commission in 1914–1915. Settler territory, I demonstrate, becomes an instrument of violence and spatialized surveillance, opening up propertied space to settlers while confining space and possibility to Indigenous people. White territories become inviolable and non-negotiable, while Indigenous territoriality is remade as contingent and permeable.

To territorialize property is to imagine it in particular ways. Chapter 5 traces the ways in which dominant understandings of property are sustained by particular conceptions of territory, as evidenced by the nostrum that 'your home is a castle'. Dominant imaginaries of property, I shall suggest, rely on the installation and defence of hard boundaries around the propertied self from which others – the state, nonowners and other owners – are to be expelled. As the self is spatialized, so is property itself. Such Blackstonian conceptions serve to reimagine property itself. Rather than a bundle of relations, 'property' itself becomes territorialized, imagined as the object of property itself. Thus it is that we commonly talk about 'buying property' or 'my property' as if it were a bounded parcel of land.

Territory does work, and such framings are of profound consequence, holding up unjust and extractive social and ecological mindsets. I demonstrate the dangerous work that this territorial logic does through an exploration of the violent and racist enforcement of the 'castle doctrine' in trespass cases, notably the widespread adoption of 'stand-your-ground' laws in the U.S. and the killing of Colten Boushie, an Indigenous man in Saskatchewan. While territorial imaginaries over-protect fee-simple owners, I also reveal the ways that those who are denied property's 'castle' – notably houseless people – face particular vulnerabilities.

While the practical and ideological work of the hegemonic forms of propertied territoriality needs to be recognized, it is important to also note the ways in which property and territory are continuously contested, reworked and sometimes remade. While this is noted throughout, the goal of Chapter 6 is to foreground contestation and alternatives. Dominant conceptions of property invite a sharp divide between insiders and outsiders. So, for example, it is easy to assume that private property (as a castle) is simply a story of rightful exclusion. This ignores the reality of property practice, however. Case law and property practice reveal that the territory of property can also be a space of conditional access. This, in part, reflects the actions of those we might term 'territory's outlaws', such as squatters, civil rights activists, sit-down strikers, Indigenous activists and houseless people. Their precarious status, in many senses, is shaped by the exclusion generated by the territorialization of dominant property relations. Their struggles, moreover, centre not only on property relations but crucially also on their territorialization.

Acknowledgments

My sincere thanks to Sam Wallman for his permission to reproduce sections of 'So below'. Thanks also to his collaborators: Nomad Projects (nomadprojects.org), Urban Mind (urbanmind.info), Phytology (phytology.org.uk) and Backyard (backyardproject.org)

I am also grateful to the participants in my Fall 2021 graduate seminar who commented on some of the chapters, namely Naomi Keenan O'Shea, Terri Evans, Bruna de Oliveira Maciel, Prem Sylvester and Irwin Oostindie.

Thanks to my friend Mariana Valverde for asking me to write this and for her constructive comments and advice. Thanks also to Alexandra Flynn and to members of the Decommission Collective (Mayana Slobodian, Sarah Hunt, Brenna Bhandar, Marianne Nicholson and Paige Raibmon). Tyler McCreary provided very useful advice regarding Indigenous resistance and territoriality.

Sections of this book draw from or reproduce earlier publications. My thanks to the publishers in all cases.

Chapter 1 draws in part from Blomley, N (2020) 'Precarious territory: Property law, housing and the social order' *Antipode* 52, 1, pp 26–57 (Wiley)

Chapter 3 draws in part from Blomley, N (2019) 'The territorialization of property in land: space, power, and practice' *Territory, politics, governance*. 72, 233–249 (Wiley), available online at www.tandfonline.com/doi/10.1080/21622671.2017.1359107; and from Blomley, N (2007) 'Making private property: enclosure, common right and the work of hedges', *Rural History*. 18, 1, 1–21 (Cambridge University Press).

Chapter 4 borrows from some ideas forthcoming in a chapter co-edited by Nicole Graham, Margaret Davies and Lee Godden (forthcoming), *Routledge Handbook of Property, Law, and Society*

Chapter 5 includes some material drawn from Blomley, N. (2020) 'Urban commoning and the right not to be excluded'. In D. Ozkan and G. B. Buyuksarac (Eds.), *Commoning the city* (pp 89–103). Routledge. Reproduced by permission of Taylor and Francis Group, LLC, a division of Informa plc

1

Territory

A forestry company, Teal Jones, acquired a licence from the government of British Columbia to cut old-growth trees from forest land designated 'Tree Farm Licence 46' (TFL 46) in southern Vancouver Island, around the watershed of Fairy Creek. A licence is a permission granted by one entity to another to do something that, without permission, would be illegal. While the state regards this as 'Crown' (government-owned) land, TFL 46 lies within the traditional territory of the Pacheedaht First Nation. Elected leaders of the Nation had negotiated a revenue sharing agreement with the province, under which they would receive a portion of the payments that Teal Jones would give to the province for the right to harvest timber (also known as stumpage rates). However, a Pacheedaht Elder, Bill Jones, opposed the plan, insisting that this ancient forest on Indigenous land should be left intact. Following his call, environmentalists established blockades, preventing access by logging crews.

On April 1 2021, the British Columbia Supreme Court granted an injunction to Teal Jones, preventing protests. The Royal Canadian Mounted Police (RCMP) subsequently established a restricted access zone around the worksite with a checkpoint. Protestors who wished to engage in peaceful protest could only do so in a designated zone. Many elected not to do so: once crossing into the access zone, they were open to arrest. As a condition of their release on bail, many were required to stay away from the protest zone.

The Fairy Creek protest continues as I write. It is about many issues, such as state sovereignty, Indigenous rights, and extractive capitalism. But it is clear that the dispute unfolds in and over land spatial access to which is governed in part by property rules. Protestors claim to be protecting Indigenous sovereignty over traditional territory by denying access to logging crews while also articulating a collective interest in old-growth forests. Teal Jones has a property interest in the trees by

DOI: 10.4324/9781003253389-1

virtue of its licence from the Crown, which claims the title. Pachee-daht Nation members variously ask the protestors to leave or invite them to participate. The RCMP seeks to uphold Teal Jones' property interest through a set of territorial controls, closely regulating who can be where. The territorial dimensions of property are central to this and many other social relationships and conflicts.

As property and territory seem like obvious concepts, so too can the relationship between the two appear straightforward. Ask laypeople to visualize 'property', and they'll probably evoke a single-family private home, possibly with a fence or hedges around it, set apart from its neighbours. Property, in this model, *is* territory. Property is a bounded piece of land that individuals control. While they may invite others to enter the garden gate, it is theirs, over which they have certain powerful rights – notably that of exclusion, whether metaphorical, spatial, or both.

This imaginary accurately describes the dominant way in which property and territory are imagined and thought about. While inaccurate, it deserves our attention. But I want us also to recognize that as property is not just a relationship to land but is inherently a relationship to others, so also territory is much more than a simple, sleepy fence or hedge. Rather, it too is relational. In other words, the way in which territory is arranged, governed, and represented is both a product of social relations, including property, and a means by which such relations are structured, experienced, imagined, and challenged. The territory of property is far from obvious or straightforward but is historically and culturally conditional, as we shall see. Rather than simply a technical arrangement, it is also deeply social in its effects, structuring deeply engrained relationships of power, privilege, and dependency.

Territory

The struggle over Fairy Creek is clearly a story about property. But as noted, it is also about the territorial dimensions of property. What do I mean by territory? I define it simply as a 'unit of contiguous space that is used, organized and managed by a social group, individual person, or institution to restrict or control spatial access to people and places' (Agnew, 2009, p. 746). Delaney (2005, p. 14) also provides a useful definition:

> A simple territory marks a differentiation between an 'inside' and an 'outside'. The meanings refer, in the first instance, to the practical significance of being on the inside or the outside or of crossing a line that distinguishes one side from the other. . . . The basics

of territory, then, are fairly straightforward: a space, a line, some meaning, some state of affairs.

(Delaney, 2005, p. 14)

Territory, therefore, has an inside and an outside. It mobilizes a set of social meanings that give this configuration some significance. Territory is socially produced to serve multiple ends. 'Social distancing' rules, which encourage people to stay away from a two-meter personal territorial bubble, are one example, while the sovereign territory of a state is another. It is worth pausing for a moment here in order to be clear regarding how I am using 'territory'. It is to be distinguished from other geographic concepts such as a 'place', for example, or a 'region'. A postal code or zip code area is not a territory, nor is a place. While bounded and used by social groups or institutions, these spaces do not necessarily govern spatial access. However, if a place becomes controlled by a criminal gang, who expel rival gang members from it, it has been territorialized.

Territory can take many forms and serve many ends. It can be highly formalized or more diffuse. It can claim to be universal in scope, like a state, or can be particular in its reach applying only to gang members. The spatial access rules governing territory can take multiple forms. They can regulate individuals, groups, or everyone. These rules may prevent spatial access or facilitate it. Commoners have the right to take a cow onto the common as long as they are members of a local village. The boundary that encompasses territory may also take many forms, from sharply demarcated lines or material objects, such as fences, to zones or even networks (Thom, 2009).

Western liberal property – my focus here – appears territorialized in a different way, tightly grounded in a bounded, exclusive space. As we shall see in Chapter 5, there is a strong functional and ideological association between private property and a sharply territorialized and often fortified space, expressed most powerfully in the idea of property as like a castle, whose boundaries defend the owner against those outside.

So powerful is this conception that it is hard to see the many different and diverse ways in which relations, particularly concerning the access or use of land, are differently territorialized. The property of territory, in other words, need not be a castle (Ingold, 1987). The Maori land system, for example, operates according to a specific territoriality, according to Banner (1999), such that 'a person would not own a zone of space; he [sic] would instead own the right to use a particular resource in a particular way' (811). Property rights in durian trees in the Indonesian rainforest may entail multiple claimants, with temporal shifts in access (Peluso, 1996).

Figure 1.1 Sharp lines.
Source: From sobelow.org; reproduced with permission.

Nor does Western property conform to a singular territorial logic. For as property serves multiple ends and takes multiple forms, including state or collective property regimes, so its territorial manifestations can be organized in diverse and often creative ways. Property boundaries are not necessarily walls, metaphorically speaking, but may serve as gateways, facilitating access and inclusion (Peñalver, 2005). Property held by the state or by collectives may have inclusive territorial rules, as evidenced by the subtle conversations around exclusion and access in public libraries (Freeman & Blomley, 2019). Private property may be territorially collectivized, as in the case of groups of property owners who combine in defence of their private interests and seek to expel the unwanted from 'their' neighbourhood. Complex territorial overlays may also be at work in denser settings – the case of privately owned public space is one example. Rather than a sharp legal line between the inside and outside of the boundary, legal practice is more graduated – an owner has a more robust right to exclude from her home than at the garden gate (Dana & Shoked, 2019). Property's territory also has a crucial temporality, maybe with different territorial rules operating at different times of the day or year and changing historically (Fisher, 2016; see Chapter 3).

We tend not to think about the relation between territory and property. My goal in this book is to challenge this oversight. But it is interesting to reflect on the gap in critical scholarship on this topic. Perhaps it reflects the ways in which both concepts tend to be conceived. As I will discuss in the following chapter, a dominant 'ownership model' tends to position property as inert, obvious, and non-political. Similarly, to think about territory is to invoke 'space'. Modernist epistemology tends to treat 'space' as an external thing, out there in the world, prior to social and political processes (Soja, 1989). Territorial manifestations of property, like the white picket fence, combining both 'space' and 'law' can thus be easily read as an arrangement of inert objects and dispassionate rules. If, as we should, we are interested in the social relationality of property, then territory is easily sidelined.

But this would be a mistake. As noted in the preface, space, and the rules that govern access to it, are of fundamental importance. We all 'take up space', and all of us need 'sum room'. Arguing from first principles, Jeremy Waldron (1991) traces the fundamental connections between space, property, and freedom. 'Everything that is to be done has to be done somewhere' (296), he notes. We are not free, therefore, unless we have a space in which we are free to perform an action, or space is regulated in such a way as to make such freedoms impossible. Property rules, he notes, 'give us a way of determining, in the case of each place, who is allowed to be in that place and who is not' (296). Private property rules are operative

> when an individual person may determine who is, and who is not, allowed to be in a certain place, without answering to anyone else for that decision. I say who is allowed to be in my house. He says who is to be allowed in his restaurant.
>
> (297)

Waldron's particular concern is for the houseless person, for whom 'there is no place governed by a private property rule where he [sic] is allowed to be ... whenever he chooses' (299). While the argument is compelling (although, compare with Blomley, 2009), it should be extended. We need to consider the complex property rules that govern us all, to varying degrees, and the ways in which they grant conditional access to 'sum room'. The freedoms of space are hedged in by property's conditionalities, such as short-term leases, mortgage endebtedness, arbitrary rent increases, predatory landlords, shelter rules, the relative tolerance of the state to informal settlements, and so on. While we are all inside the territory of property, in this sense, we are also differently positioned. Property's territoriality holds some up while holding and confining others to more liminal and precarious spaces. The manner in which property is territorialized, therefore, implicates fundamental questions of freedom.

To ignore territory would be a mistake in a second sense. To treat property as somehow pre-political is, I argue later, misguided. Similarly, geographers argue that spaces, such as territory, are both a social product and constitutive of social relations (Painter, 2010). The meanings we attach to space, and the way we arrange spaces, entail human action. These practices are not simply individual but are organized at a social or collective level – hence we can talk of the social production of space. But a space is not simply a social outcome. It is also generative. The space of a lecture theatre, for example, shapes a set of social activities and relationships about the power and authority of a professor, centred on the room relative to that of a student, positioned as passive recipients.

Similarly, I encourage us in this chapter to think about territory not as an external thing but as both a product of property and as a means by which property relations are enacted and sustained, in partnership with other legal practices, notably sovereignty (Blomley, 2016a). How might we do this? As a first cut, we might consider that in an everyday sense, we meet the abstraction that is 'property' in and through its territorial manifestations. These territorial arrangements may give us comfort and security, or they may be expulsive and extractive. These territorial manifestations are varied and diverse. Some of these are material, embodied, or practical, and others are more representational. Some are the domain of 'Law' and sustained by social force and violence, while others are expressions of lived legality. Property relations, therefore, are often experienced, judged, enacted, and contested in and through these territorial encounters. Here are a few of them:

a. Perhaps most immediately, we encounter the territorial dimensions of property rules through legally consequential *material arrangements*, like walls, doors, and fences. The barbed wire fence or the garden hedge are obvious materializations of private property and, in some cases, state property. Such lumpish things seem obvious by the quotidian ubiquity. But their very materiality may prove more complicated: fences and hedges can serve multiple material ends, reflecting the varied valences of property. In the traditional commons, for example, fences and hedges were often used to contain (animals, in particular) rather than to exclude. With enclosure, however, hedges and fences were used both symbolically and practically to exclude commoners and their animals from accessing land that had now been privatized, as discussed in Chapter 3.

b. We also perform property's territory through *everyday spatial practices*, such as walking, gardening, and looking. Such practices may inscribe territorial rules, as we stay on the designated footpath and avoid the temptation to graze from our neighbour's vegetable patch. But we can also remake territorial arrangements through such practices. By routinely walking along a given route, for example, a right of way can be carved out of an otherwise exclusive territory through the doctrine of prescriptive right. But routine spatial practices can also bump up against the remaking of property's territory. Raja Shehadeh (2008) documents the manner in which his much-loved hill walks around his home in Ramallah in the Palestinian West Bank are increasingly hedged in by the territorial property claims of Israeli settlers.

c.   Property's territory also comes to us *visually*. It is no surprise that the cover of Carol Rose's magisterial collection of essays on property shows a gate and fence. Sight, she notes, 'dominates the persuasive and rhetorical aspects of property' (1994, p. 267). As we are invited to summon images of objects (like bundles of sticks) to think about property, so too does property's territory come to us through particular visualizations. Maps, in particular, are a powerful means by which property spaces are represented (Pottage, 1994). But as vision is a complicated process, so maps come with strings attached.

d.   Property is an act of imagination and belief. The stories we are told and tell ourselves of property often turn on territorial norms and conceptions. So it is that property's territory is also expressed in *everyday tropes and imaginaries*. For example, in Anglo culture, it is commonplace to liken the home to a castle. To do so, as I discuss in Chapter 5, is to invoke an important set of territorial framings of property, the individual, and the collective. Castles, of course, are to be defended.

e.   We may also invoke property's territory through *legal practices*, like evictions, trespass, licences, and easements. This, of course, is partly the domain of formal legal practice. Property disputes often turn on questions relating to territoriality or on the adjudication of who can be where relative to a given set of territorial arrangements. But a deeply territorialized concept such as trespass constitutes powerful understandings of placement, morality, and right, as I note later.

f.   Property is deeply imbued with a set of organizing frameworks and *norms*, many of them territorial. The concept of 'improvement', for example, is deeply tied both to racialized notions of propertied personhood and presumptions of territorial exclusivity. To improve is to be white and to be fenced, put bluntly. John Winthrop, the first Governor of the Massachusetts Bay Colony, asserted that as the 'Natives in New England . . . inclose noe land' and have no means by which 'to improve the Land', it followed that their land 'lay open to any that could and would improve it' (Fields, 2017, p. xii).

Property's territory comes to us in many ways, therefore. How might we begin to think more systematically about territory then? I think one useful approach, following Brighenti, is to recognize that it is 'better conceived as an art or practice rather than an object or physical space' (2010a, p. 53). As property produces and polices the connections and distinctions of social life, so also can we see territory as an 'interaction device' (Brighenti, 2010b, p. 224) that helps organize the relations inherent to the production of property, establishing a particular 'economy of objects and places' (Brighenti, 2006, p. 75). Territorialization helps to define, inscribe, and stabilize a set of relations (Brighenti, 2010b, p. 223) associated with property. Territory, in turn, is produced and shaped by property's practices.

The question thus becomes

> what can be grasped by describing something [in our case, property] – and, specifically, a series of relational phenomena rather than a series of objects – as a territory, and what can one learn on law [notably property] by looking at it as a territorial endeavour?
> (Brighenti, 2006, p. 66)

Drawing from the territorial encounters noted previously, what particular work does territory do in regard to property relations, and with what consequences?

a.   *Communication*: Robert Sack (1986, p. 21) notes that 'the territorial boundary may be the only symbolic form that combines direction in space and a statement about possession or exclusion'. Territory – particularly its material markers – structures property relations through communicating the social meanings that are attached to it. These territorial meanings are rich and varied.

It is the presumptive communicative obviousness of property boundaries that make them particularly useful, some argue. This is important in that property is an 'in rem' right which applies not to a specified audience (such as a contract, which binds only designated people) but to the world at large. As such, communication becomes a challenge. The advantage of territory is that, generally speaking, its meanings are said to be clearly legible to others. Henry Smith (2014) argues that the potential complexity of property relations are short-circuited through the use of territorial boundaries, communicating clear messages to duty-bearers. The person who encounters the boundary fence need not know anything about the person who owns the land behind it – whether she is virtuous, whether the land is leased or held by an aboriginal community and so on. All she needs to know, Smith (2014) argues, is that it does not belong to her.

Yet such meanings may not be so straightforward. They have to be learned; thus it is that we spend a lot of time instructing children in the meanings of property boundaries. Children's literature teaches the young that Peter Rabbit is naughty because he has climbed under Mr. McGregor's fence. He has crossed a boundary, clearly marked with fences, gates, and so on, moving from an 'outside' into an 'inside'. Following Locke, Mr. McGregor has clearly mixed his labour with the soil by intensively gardening the site and thus improving it in a way that Locke would approve of. He exercises his right to exclude, central to property. Peter Rabbit, who is 'very naughty', is appropriately punished for his transgression.

However, as communication is not a straightforward act, so territory can be read differently, misread, or simply ignored. Colonial dispossession relies on a selective misreading of another culture's territorial markers. Communicative markers that signalled people's relation to land and to others were either illegible within Western cultural registers or were simply ignored (Cronon, 2003)

Moreover, the meanings of territory are not simply factual: rather, they come ethically charged (Mitchell, 2015). Take trespass, for example. Hayes (2020, p. 18) characterizes this word as one of the most charged in the English language,

> wrapped in a moral stigma that runs to the heart of . . . political and civil life. Many of our liberties and the restrictions on them are expressed in terms of land, parameters, and property, so much so that it is hard to tell which is a metaphor for the others.

To 'cross the line', to be 'beyond the pale', to challenge 'personal space', and 'acceptable boundaries' all signal a profound departure from established norms. A 'deviant' is someone who has strayed from a path. 'Trespass' itself, Hayes (2020) notes, is etymologically linked to transgression: hence it is that Christians pray for God to 'forgive us our trespasses'.

b. *Enforcement*: To territorialize property relations is also to facilitate and frame the enforcement of property. A person's position relative to a property boundary serves as a visible marker that can trigger a legal response. Law, it should be remembered, is an organized form of sanctioned violence, realized or implied (Blomley, 2003). Etymologically, territory derives from the Latin 'terra' (earth) and 'terrere' (to frighten). Territory, literally put, is land from which people are to be frightened away. For most of us, protected by property's territoriality, its violences are muted. However, for those who live more precariously, the violences of territory are clearly evident.

Take, for example, the actions of eviction and trespass. Banal and omnipresent, they serve as the backstop to a prevailing property regime. If exclusion is the *sine qua non* of private property (Merrill, 1998), then they serve as its essential instruments. Both can entail forms of violence. Both are distinctively territorial.

In Chapter 5, I consider the particular territorial logic of trespass, which has been redefined over time such that a generalized wrong becomes understood as the crossing of a property boundary. Eviction also needs to be understood as deeply territorial, both in its effect and rationale. It rests on the territorialized concept of exclusive possession, defined as a 'conclusion of law defining the nature and status of a particular relationship of control by a person over land' (Gray & Gray, 2009, p. 105). Possession is thus understood as a straightforward expression of territorial control. In the common law, the quantum of property which a person has in land is measured by his ability to vindicate his [sic] sovereign control over territorial space' (ibid.). Property, from this perspective, 'consists primarily in control over access'.[1] Leasehold and freehold are thus strongly associated 'with a powerful . . . sense of territorial belonging and overall control. Both estates resonate with significant sovereignty over terrain' (Gray & Gray, 2009, p. 164).

If property entails 'control over access' and 'sovereignty over terrain', it follows that eviction should be understood as realizing the absolute expulsion of people and their possessions from a territory to which they cannot return without the permission of the owner. The sharply territorialized logic of eviction is revealed in its euphemisms: to be 'put out', to 'get the boot', to 'get the bum's rush', or to be 'bounced'. Eviction is a naked form of territorialized legal power premised on a precarious property relation. The most effective way to enact the ownership of land, Desmond (2016, p. 45) notes, 'is to force people from it'.

But property's territorial rules can also be enforced to open up territory, as I note in Chapter 6. Property is not just a space from which others are to be excluded. Rules may be enforced that open up even

---

1 *Yanner v. Eaton* (1999) 201 CLR 251.

privatized resources, for example. Depoorter (2011), echoing the 'fair use' principle applied to intellectual property, goes so far as to argue for a 'fair trespass' proposal that seeks to balance 'the privilege of exclusion against the interests in access' (1100).

c. *Imagination:* 'Territory does much of our thinking for us', notes Delaney (2005, p. 18); it becomes 'a way of seeing' (Brighenti, 2006, p. 69). As such, territorial frameworks shape how we conceive property relations. Consider, for example, the way in which trespass is understood. Formally, it is governed by tort law, a form of private law that regulates interactions not governed by contract. 'Tort' denotes injuries upon the person, such as assaults, negligent acts, and defamation. That trespass is a tort presumes that a person's territorial boundaries are an extension of their self: 'To step over the line into private property is, in the eyes of the law, not an act of digression but of aggression, and makes the landowner the victim' (Hayes, 2020, p. 326).

But territory may be even more profound as a way of seeing property. Lawyers often get annoyed when laypeople talk of property as if it were a parcel of land. To buy or sell property is to trade in such parcels. 'Property', in other words, is imagined as if it were an inert space rather than a bundle of territorialized relations. But such a conception, while technically wrong, nevertheless accurately represents dominant ideologies that strip property of relationality and imagine it as reified space.

But it is not simply the objects of property that are territorialized. The possessive individual, central to private property, is also spatialized, imagined as a presocial, autonomous, and distinctive subject, protected from others by the shield of rights (Nedelsky, 1989, 1990). Property thus becomes a boundary marking off the legal subject. It is no accident that property talk is replete with spatial metaphors when it comes to describing the individuated legal subject.

It is in this light, perhaps, that we can understand the tendency to naturalize a particular view of property and territory. As property and territory appear unchanging and thing-like, so also is it appealing to imagine that exclusive territorialized possession is somehow hardwired in human societies, overlooking the highly contingent nature of both private property and territory (see Chapter 3). Take, for example, Pipes (1999) highly deterministic reading of (private) property and the apparently natural tendency of people to carve out exclusive territory. Thus, he argues, '[a]s in the case of animals, the leading causes of human acquisitiveness are economic and biological: the need of territory and of objects with which to sustain oneself and procreate' (71). Children are argued to reflect an inherent pre-political possessiveness: 'Empirical studies have . . . demonstrated that in order to develop normally, children, like animals, require a certain amount of private space' (75). Quoting Bruno Bettelheim, Pipes goes on to argue that 'territorial demarcation' is necessary for children's psychic health.

d. *Ideology*: The imaginaries of property, of course, are thus far from neutral. The metaphors through which we think can constrain as much as they make possible. Similarly, the territorial imaginary does ideological work as well. Squeezing private property relations and obligations through a narrow territorial frame obscures, normalizes, and legitimizes the social violences endemic to property. To the extent that territory is reified as a thing, it depersonalizes property relations, such that territory 'appears as the agent doing the controlling' (Sack, 1983, p. 59) rather than the social relations that sustain exclusion. Private property thus appears not to be about social relations of power and force but about abstract 'spaces' and 'boundaries'.

The territorial framing of the subject and object of property noted previously is deeply consequential, shaping ethical deliberation and engagement with others, as the metaphors of 'distant strangers' and those 'nearest and dearest' hint at. The drawing of metaphoric boundaries invites an ethic of entitlement, rather than one of obligation, exemplified by the small-minded neighbour who 'moves in darkness' in Robert Frost's poem 'Mending Wall'. As a consequence, it becomes easier to view the houseless person outside my gate as a threat to my property rather than someone whose very location is a product of my own good fortune. Imagined thus, the solution to his or her troubling presence is some form of removal. Such ideological territorializations can thus do violent work (see figure 1.2).

e. *Performance*: Property and territory are best thought of not as static products but as social performances, continuously put to work to achieve various social ends (Blomley, 2013). Yet performances of any sort are always incomplete, potentially unstable, and contestable. Dominant arrangements of property, because of their importance to social life and possibility, are contested, reworked, and sometimes remade, sometimes in the service of subaltern property systems (Blomley, 2013).

Figure 1.2 'Like a hot knife thru butter'.
Source: From sobelow.org; reproduced with permission.

So, for example, the communicative messages of property's territorializations are capable of alternative readings. Peter Rabbit may be a trespasser, formally speaking, but surely many readers celebrate his transgressive pluck. Contrary to Smith's (2014) assertions regarding the modular simplicity of property boundaries, people read the boundaries between them and their neighbours or the public with far more complexity and nuance (Blomley, 2016b). The imaginaries of territorialized property can be more diverse than the certainties of the castle metaphor. Oppositional groups, such as squatters, strikers, civil rights campaigners, right-to-roam activists, travellers, Indigenous Nations, and homeless activists, routinely contest dominant property arrangements, including their territorial expressions, appealing to the oppressions that such geographies create and articulating alternative entitlements to land and resources. Their precarious status, in many senses, is shaped by the exclusion generated in part by property's territory. Their struggles, moreover, centre not only on property relations but crucially also on their territorial form.

2

Property

The struggle over Fairy Creek, introduced in Chapter 1, is deeply territorial. Yet, at stake are multiple conflicting interests in the land. Some of these (Crown title, a timber lease) are formalized and upheld by the state. While others are a little harder to discern, they are no less important. In defending an old-growth forest, protestors assert a collective or common property interest in the trees. Pacheedaht Nation's revenue sharing agreement is grounded in aboriginal title to the land – long denied, this is now increasingly recognized by the courts as a (more-or-less) legitimate property interest. However, other members of the Pacheedaht Nation – notably Elder Bill Jones – articulate a claim to the land based on Indigenous law and sovereignty, denying Crown title and sovereignty. To understand this conflict, and social relations more generally, we need to understand these interests in the land.

It is necessary, then, to think more carefully about property. As noted, however, the tendency is to think that property, like territory, is obvious. This reflects the dominance of an 'ownership model' that shapes our understanding of what property actually is and how it should be structured (Blomley, 2004). The ownership model is present in popular discourse, academic argument, and judicial decision-making:

> What is property? One might think this was a simple question. Property is about rights over things and the people who have those rights are called owners. What powers do owners have over the things they own? Owners are free to use the property as they wish. They have the right to exclude others from it or grant them access over it. They have the power to transfer title – to pass the powers of ownership to someone else. They are also immune from having the property taken away from them without their consent,

DOI: 10.4324/9781003253389-2

or they must be adequately compensated if the property is taken by the state for public purposes.

(Singer, 2000, pp. 2–3)

According to the ownership model, property is reduced to private property – the two become synonymous. Property is also reified. It is imagined as 'about rights over things'. It assumes a single owner identifiable by formal title rather than informal or moral claims. The owner is assumed to be motivated by self-interested and self-regarding behaviour: for example, improving the land in order to attain a higher resale price. The owner is metaphorically set against other interests, who are seen as threats – notably the state. While state intervention can occur, this is always suspect and must be justified in relation to the prior and superior rights of the owner. Property rights protect us, as individuals, from the collective.

The ownership model also privileges the exclusionary powers that private property owners have. Indeed, for some commentators, property requires exclusion for it to function. William Blackstone famously characterized property rights as 'that sole and despotic dominion which one man claims and exercises over the external things of the world, in total exclusion of the rights of any other individual in the universe' (1766/1979a, p. 2). 'Give someone the right to exclude others from a valued resource. . ., and you give them property', argued Merrill; '[d]eny someone the exclusion right and they do not have property' (1998, p. 730). Historically, these exclusionary powers have been celebrated. Supposedly, exclusion provides incentives for individuals to work, encourages improvement, and minimizes wasteful disputes (Ellickson, 1993, p. 1322).

The ownership model, I shall argue, is empirically inaccurate and ethically incomplete (Blomley, 2004; Singer, 2000). It misdescribes the actual workings of property while short-circuiting an analysis of its social effects. It treats the inherently social and political relationality of property as a purely individualistic and 'private' matter, obscuring the central role of the collective in defining the property bundle. Its logic of exclusion overlooks the crucial role of property in organizing inclusion. Its value monism ignores property's ethical pluralism. It also misconceives the work of territory.

So what might a better account of property look like? One introductory definition thinks of property as a system of rules governing people's access to and use of valued resources. As a system of rules, property, therefore, necessarily entails interactions between people.

These rules can be arranged in multiple ways. One way to distinguish these arrangements is to ask whose wishes and needs are to be central – the individual, the collective, or all members of a society or group (Waldron, 1990)? Under a private property system, resources are assigned to singular individuals. Under private property rules,

> a norm is established that, in the case of each object, the individual person whose name is attached to it shall determine how that object is to be used, and by whom. His [sic] decision is to be upheld by society as final.
>
> (Waldron, 1990, p. 39)

However, it is also often decided that the use of certain resources is to be determined by reference to the collective interests of society rather than an individual, as in the case of state property. Further, it might be determined that a resource is available for members of a specific group rather than any individual or the collective: this is common property. Property can take many forms, in other words, and should not be reduced simply to private property.

At minimum, if a property system assigns rights to a particular resource to an individual or group, it follows that others' rights to that resource are to be limited. Even this limited treatment, therefore, begins to direct us to the relationality of property. Property is clearly about rights over things, but those things are only governed by property rules when they are valued by others. Property rules would make no sense if I were the only person interested in a resource. There are few property rules governing oxygen, for example, because it is widely available, and my use does not subtract from yours. When a resource is of interest to others, property structure sanctioned rules between people regarding a resource. So, for example, a private property rule would allow an individual owner to determine who may use a resource and under what conditions. She may choose to allow others to share in that resource or may decline access to others.

Furthermore, property rules can be said to be relational in that they require a collective agency or a state. This land is mine not because of the labour I mixed with it but because the state says it's mine. 'What I own depends on what you agree that I own, not what I assert that I own', notes Bromley (1998, p. 25). Put another way, property rights are a delegation of sovereign power (Cohen, 1927). Property is thus 'derived from sovereignty, but also creates sovereignty' (Singer, 1991, p. 51). If property can be imagined as like a

defensive space (see Chapter 5), we must not forget that '[o]ur reg-
ulations . . . shape the house that we live in, and the liberty that
we value comes from having built that house and the environment
around it' (Singer, 2008, p. 141).

Property is also relational in terms of the values it serves and must be
justified by such ends. Now, there is a strong tendency to assume that a
singular value – such as utility or autonomy – is sustained by property.
However, such a monist perspective evident in the ownership model,
is inadequate. Property values are inherently pluralist, Alexander and
Peñalver (2012) point out. This is partly so by virtue of the multiple
social-relational contexts in which property is present. Values such as
individual autonomy – valid in some contexts – do not translate easily
in the context of marital property, for example, in which values such
as sharing make more sense. Property values are also dynamic and historical. The history of private property reveals not only individualistic
values but also the enduring presence of 'proprietarian' norms that
hold that property is meant not simply to satisfy individual prefer-
ences 'but to fulfill some prior normative vision of how society and
the polity that governs it should be structured' (Alexander, 1997, p. 2;
Blomley, 2005). When we move beyond private property, as we must,
we also encounter other justifiable values. Public property, for example,
may seek to uphold sociability, public belonging, and tolerance (Page,
2021). The diversity of the resources governed by property rules also
means a diversity of property values are likely to be at stake. Some may
be framed as market commodities, valued for their capacity to generate
wealth. Others may be valued for their ability to contribute to shared
memories and identity. Such values also change depending on who
holds a resource. A family home likely embodies different values to a
developer than to its occupants.

Property is thus inherently social, not narrowly individualistic,
reflecting and constituting social relations (Davies, 2007). This becomes
particularly clear in relation to property in land, my focus here. If we
take the relationality of property seriously, we are obliged to recognize
that property is not simply one of insiders and outsiders but rather
structures a complex set of organized relationships and rights. There is
no outside to property, in other words. We all access property in land
in and through legally situated others, but we do so under differently
calibrated terms. This can be through the permission or contractual
agreement of others, such as the lease of an apartment. It can also
occur through the staged concessions or forced compliance of others, as in colonial relations. All settlers access land through a relation

with Indigenous societies, the original owners of the land, although on highly unequal terms. While access through others is obvious in the case of those such as renters, mobile home park residents, or homeless people camping on state property, it is also evident in the case of those with apparently more secure entitlements, such as the homeowner, who may require a relationship with a mortgagee, or the state.

Use and access of land for shelter are thus conditional on relations with others. Such relations implicate both parties in ways that can be mutual and extractive. In some cases, it can entail formal obligations, such as the requirement that public land serves public ends, or the treaty obligations that settler societies should have with Indigenous peoples (Pasternak, 2017). Property is thus a relational meshwork in which we are all variously positioned. For better or worse, as workers, Indigenous persons, tenants, condo owners, or homeless people, we are all entangled within property. This is why property is so important: it can neither be willed away, as some critics suppose, nor mythologized as an egalitarian form of horizontal mutuality, as private property proponents insist.

Property law is a means by which this codependency is organized. While law facilitates exclusion, it also encourages the collective access and use of space via easements, public trust doctrine, commoning, condominium law, landlord–tenant law, and so on.

In that property rules structure relations between people in regards to a valued resource such as land, property is grounded on and helps create forms of social power. Property rules determine who can and who can't use and access certain vital resources, like land. Because property is a relation between people, this means that those who are empowered by property rules have power over other people. If I own a resource like urban land that others need, I am legally empowered (more or less) to decide how that land will be used and by whom. I might choose to exclude others from that land or allow others to access my land under conditions I get to choose (for example, by renting it out to tenants).

Property is best described, therefore, as 'simply the word used to describe particular concentrations of powers over things' (Gray & Gray, 2009, p. 90), operative between persons (Hallowell, 1943, pp. 119–120) creating complex relations of dependence, sovereignty, and privilege. Property is a social institution that involves multiple people, all with interests in a valued resource. When we organize and distribute property rights, in other words, we necessarily allocate and enforce social privileges and resources. Property rights, in that sense, are 'collective, enforced, even violent decisions about who shall enjoy the privileges and resources which this society allocates among its citizens' (Under-kuffler, 2003, p. 146).

In modern, liberal, capitalist societies, such decisions often privilege owners over non-owners. As the legal realist Morris Cohen pointed out nearly a century ago, the private property rights of the owner confer power over others:

> If . . . somebody else wants to use the food, the house, the land, or the plough that the law calls my own, he [sic] has to get my consent. To the extent that these things are necessary to the life of my neighbour, the law thus confers on me a power, limited but real, to make him do what I want. . . . *Dominion* over things is also *imperium* over our fellow human beings.
>
> (Cohen, 1927, pp. 12–13)

Put another way, a property regime structures interlocking relations of power and vulnerability:

> 'The freedom to use or possess limited resources implies a cor-relative vulnerability in others. The failure to assign an exclusive property right to a specific person leaves her at risk of having her interests infringed by others'
>
> (Singer, 1991, p. 41).

Consider the power granted to landlords relative to tenants, allowing landowners to assert their rights to exclusive possession by evicting anyone who cannot prove a stronger right in defence. Depending on the jurisdiction, the right to evict may be exercised without any reference to contextual factors, such as the general socio-political context or the personal circumstances of the occupier.

> (van der Walt, 1999)

Property rules, therefore, are not neutral but serve to create forms of power between differently placed subjects. The ability to exercise 'imperium' via 'dominion', in other words, is not random but socially structured and organized:

> property rights are not self-defining. Rather, the legal system makes constant choices about which interests to define as property. It also determines how to allocate power between competing claimants

when interests conflict. And the pattern of protection and vulnerability is a result of a historical and social context which has created different opportunities based on such factors as race, sex, sexual orientation, disability and class.

(Singer, 1991, p. 47)

Take race, for example, a theme to which I return in more detail in Chapter 4. Indigenous peoples in British Columbia, Canada, were denied the right to pre-empt or homestead their own land on the presumption that they were racially incapable of improving it. One government official described them in 1865 as 'a vagrant people who live by fishing, hunting, and bartering skins; and the cultivation of their ground contributes [only] a few days digging of wild roots' (in Begg 2007, p. 51). Japanese Canadian property owners were stripped of their real and personal property in the 1940s in pursuit of white supremacist exclusion (Stanger-Ross, 2020).

Property is thus also relational in that it holds up systemic forms of social privilege and domination, valuing some lives while devaluing others (Dorries, 2022). Racialized relationships of dominance and vulnerability have clearly shaped property rules and practices, further inscribing racial hierarchies and geographies and associated differential access to wealth and resources (Best & Ramirez, 2021). People and communities are differentially positioned to benefit from a property system by virtue of their racialized status. But property is not simply shaped by race; property also constitutes racial hierarchies (Berger, 2021). Brenna Bhandar (2018) demonstrates how Western property law has evolved through the colonial encounter and the associated formation of racial subjects, legitimizing colonial settler practices while racializing those deemed unfit to own property.

Given this, how might we trace more carefully the work of property in organizing social relations? The work of the legal realist Robert Hale (1943; see also Cockburn, 2018; Cohen, 1927) subsequently developed within critical legal studies (notably Anonymous, 1994; Kennedy, 1991; Singer, 1991) is helpful here. We can also learn from more recent property theorists, attentive to property's relationality, particularly Cooper (2007) and Keenan (2015). They help us think about how property law organizes the transactional settings in which people necessarily find themselves, vis-à-vis others, seeking access to vital socio-spatial resources, such as shelter. I call this relational complex the *property space*, suggesting that it helps us understand the work of property law in framing 'the positional power that a person occupies in the transactions through which she lives' (Anonymous, 1994, pp. 875–876). At minimum, the property space situates the participants in any relation, specifies what the participants can do to each other, frames alternatives to transacting, and communicates powerful meanings to the participants. Put more bluntly, the property space engages in naming, acting, bounding, and speaking.

Naming

Property rules assign standing to the participants in any property relationship, determining their relative status, as well as excluding those without standing in any legal context (Kennedy, 1991). The process I term naming is of profound consequence, as the relative status of 'landlord', 'tenant', or 'licensee' reveal. Of crucial significance is how law creates the 'owner' by constituting the person with the highest quantum of legal power in relation to any resource, then situating others in relation to this presumed centrality. To be legally 'named' as owner, therefore, is to be granted considerable social powers, as Singer notes:

> If 'property is a set of social relations among human beings', the legal definition of those relationships confers – or withholds – power over others. The grant of a property right to one person leaves others vulnerable to the will of the owner. Conversely, the refusal to grant a property right leaves the claimant vulnerable to the will of others, who may with impunity infringe on the interests which have been denied protection.

> (1991, p. 41)

The status of owner, however, is not pre-given. The critical question becomes: 'who can *count* as the subject who can claim home and land?' (Roy, 2017, p. A10, my emphasis). Historically, certain categories of people – women and racialized people in particular – were formally excluded from the status of 'owner'. Deemed non-persons, legally speaking, their property interests were to be governed by men, as in the case of 'couverture', or framed as objects of property, as in the case of chattel slavery. Property law and justifications of property ownership continue to be articulated through the attribution of value to the lives of those defined as having capacity and will, which is indelibly framed by classed, gendered, and racialized conceptions of the human (Byrd et al., 2018; Walcott, 2021). Cheryl Harris (1993), for example, documents how concepts of race combine with understandings of property in the United States. More than simply serving as a basis upon which the bodies of one racialized group and the lands of another could become property, her argument is that whiteness becomes an analogue of property itself.

Acting

The property space also prescribes what the designated participants in any property space can do with and do to one another or to the objects of property and under what conditions: this can be thought of as the power of 'acting'. The property space may authorize some to harm the interests of others, allowing them to call upon the violent capacities of the state to control the behaviour of others if needed. A landlord can evict tenants, for example, but a tenant cannot evict a landlord.

To be counted an owner, in particular, is to be granted considerable powers to act relative to others. A Victorian landowner, the 15th Earl of Derby, candidly listed the five main benefits of land ownership:

> 'One, political influence; two, social importance, founded on territorial possession, the most visible and unmistakeable form of wealth; three, power over tenantry; four, residential enjoyment, including what is called sport; five, the money return – the rent'.
> (quoted in Shrubsole, 2019, p. 79)

Let us take the 'money return – the rent'. As the Earl of Derby noted, this flows from private property. Landowners have both the ability and right to charge a third party rent for using their land. David Harvey characterized rent as 'a transfer payment realized through the monopoly power over land and resources conferred by the institution of private property'. In its simplest form, it is a 'payment made by a user for the privilege of using a scarce productive resource which is owned by somebody else' (1974, p. 240). '[A]irbrushed from modern economic theory' (Shrubsole, 2019, p. 25), the right to extract rent remains fundamental to social and economic relationships, generating stark and growing inequalities between a powerful rentier class able to exercise 'power over tenantry' and a growing population of renters.

Like price, it is tempting to think of rent in reductionist terms. But it must be conceived relationally as a form of 'acting' that is enabled by the property space. Most immediately, it allows one party to extract wealth from another through a process that has been described as 'value grabbing' (Andreucci et al., 2017). The terms under which value is grabbed are structured by a prevailing property space. These must be tied to other relational enactments, notably eviction. In a detailed study of slumlords in low-income rental markets in Milwaukee, Desmond (2016) demonstrates the interlocking work of rent and eviction within the property space. Rental housing is cheap to buy, and rental returns are good. Landlords do not need to invest in maintaining buildings. Rental extraction is backstopped by the power of the owner to evict the tenant. As Desmond notes, 'the most effective way to assert, or reassert ownership of land is to force people from it' (2016, p. 45). The reality and the immanent possibility of eviction serve to sustain this extractive ecology: 'The power to dictate who could stay and who must go; the power to expel or forgive: it was an old power, and it was not without caprice' (2016, p. 129). This discretionary power casts a long shadow over landlord-tenant relations. For example, tenants do not dare complain to landlords regarding housing conditions, as this might trigger eviction. Rather than simply a story of 'bad' landlords, the landlord's extractive power is a function of how the property space structures the power to act. As van der Walt (2009, p. 73) argues, the normal enforcement of property law 'will therefore more often than not privilege the protection of existing rights and result in more or less mechanical eviction of unlawful occupiers'.

Bounding

Bounding refers to the degree to which alternatives to transacting are opened or foreclosed, thus determining participants' relative staying power or their capacity to threaten or opt not to enter into any given transaction at all. In Milwaukee, poor Black households have very few private shelter options other than those provided by predatory landlords. However, if a tenant had access to non-commodified housing (for example, state housing), they could choose to opt-out of this extractive relationship. But such options are often unavailable. The 'right to buy' in the United Kingdom saw a massive 70% decline in public-owned housing, which, while not exempt from tenancy law, nevertheless offers a vital respite from the predations of Rachmanite landlords (Christophers, 2018). Echoing the earlier discussion, bounding often has a territorial dimension, closing off particular spaces – for example, by enforcing or extinguishing common rights to access land or providing or privatizing non-market housing – and thus forcing the vulnerable into precarious property relations, such as the private rental sector.

Forms of legal action, noted previously, play a role in bounding certain types of property. The introduction of settler-colonialism in British Columbia, for example, was dependent on the disciplinary and highly territorial work of property law, notably trespass, in structuring everyday Indigenous movement, as we shall see in Chapter 4. It was not agents of the state but the vigilant and watchful eyes of nearby property owners or leaseholders, backed by the law, who 'turned Native people into trespassers' (Harris, 2003, p. 271) on their own lands. The effect is to force Indigenous people into a constrained and precarious set of legal settings – either the reserve, owned by the state, or the vagaries of the settler housing market – while opening up space for settler property relations.

Talking

The property space is also highly discursive, affirming certain property positions while denigrating others. Consider the manner in which the property precariat is regarded. Renters, for example, have long been regarded as incomplete and deformed owners, alerting us to the crucial link between property and personhood (Roy, 2017). Consider also how private owners are routinely affirmed as living in 'homes' located in 'residential communities', while renters live in 'units of housing' or 'projects' that are, if anything, a threat to community (Krueckeberg, 1999). Esther Sullivan's (2018) important work on mobile home parks is instructive here. The single largest source of unsubsidized affordable housing in the US, many mobile homes are owned by their occupants while situated on land owned by others. However, powerful stigmatizing 'trailer trash' discourses that 'position the mobile home park as a marginalized and substandard community form' (945), ensuring 'a separate, secondary, and dehumanized social status for mobile home residents' (950) is at work. Such marginalizing language clearly has powerful material effects.

The property space, then, plays an important work in structuring the relationality of property. At minimum, the work of naming, acting, bounding, and talking can have significant effects. In organizing property relations, it structures interlocking relations of power and vulnerability. The social powers I gain from ownership must be linked to the precarity of nonowners. In extractive markets, rent creates poverty, as it creates wealth.

However, the property space is not a given but a product of social struggle. It emerges with and through histories of colonialism, racialization, and capitalism. It is grounded in and productive of ongoing, violent forms of relationality, notably through the devaluing of oppressed subjects, who are granted fewer relational powers, and at an extreme, becoming objects of property themselves (Bhandar, 2018; Byrd et al., 2018; Lancione, 2020). Social movements know only too well the importance of the property space in structuring the relational politics of land (see Chapter 6). The specification of the participants in a property relation, the interactions that are permitted or excluded, the alternatives to transacting, and the meanings assigned to property are historic sites of struggle, as evidenced in struggles to have Indigenous relationships to land recognized within settler legal systems (Blomley, 2015), battles around rent, or the relative power of the landlord to evict (Blackmar, 1989), the ontological standing of racialized and marginalized property subjects (Bhandar, 2018), predatory mortgage relations (D'Adda et al., 2018), squatting (Vasudevan, 2017), and so on.

The property space is a metaphorical geography, an imaginary site through which differently positioned social subjects interact and negotiate the terms by which they can access and use land. Yet there is a more immediate geography at work here relating to territory. I have pointed to some of these territorial dimensions here, but we can also bring to bear the territorialized enactments of property noted in the previous chapter – communication, enforcement, imagination, ideology, and performance. All of these are integral to the workings of property, either directly present in the property space (enforcement, for example) or framing the particular work of naming, acting, bounding, and talking.

In what follows, I hope to make the connections between property and territory clearer. To do this, it is useful to first understand the historical coevolution of our modern concepts of property and territory. This is my task in the next chapter, as I focus on modern English enclosure, when the contemporary hegemonic territorialization of property emerged. As an interaction device, territory helped reconstitute changing property relations, producing new social gradients premised on differential access and use of land. The associated resistance to enclosure was targeted both at property and territory, reflecting the manner in which their combination served to socially differentiate. For to remake property relations is to remake territory and, in so doing, to remake society. I follow this to trace the racial logics that subtend the remaking of property and territory in the fourth chapter, with a focus on colonial (re)settlement in British Columbia, Canada. Colonial settlement, I argued, entails the simultaneous remaking of property relations and the inauguration of a territorial grid that serves both practically and ideologically to rework social relations to land. Predicated on racialized notions of the human, property's territoriality was, and continues to be, weaponized by settlers. This process relied upon particular cultural imaginaries of property's territoriality. The fifth chapter notes the work of one powerful territorialized trope of property – the idea of private property as a castle. The effect, I argue, is to spatialize entitlements and obligations in highly constrained ways. Empowering owners, the effects of this trope can be devastating, I argue. Finally, as the property space is contested, so are its territorial dimensions. Property's territoriality continues to be remade – both judicially and practically – by 'territory's outlaws', such as squatters, civil rights activists, sit-down strikers, Indigenous activists, and houseless people. Their precarious status, in many senses, is shaped by the exclusion generated by the territorialization of dominant property relations. Their struggles, moreover, centre both on property relations and their territorialization.

3

Making the territory of property

It is easy to think that property and its territorial manifestations – the 'grids of straight lines laid over the round earth' – have always been with us. But that would be a mistake. The territory of property – particularly private property – within which we live is a social and historical product. The (re)making of property relations entails the (re)making of territory, both practically and imaginatively.

GRIDS OF STRAIGHT LINES
LAID OVER THE ROUND EARTH

IN ORDER TO
SOLIDIFY
PROPERTY
OWNERSHIP.

Figure 3.1 'Grids of straight lines'.
Source: From sobelow.org; reproduced with permission.

This chapter tracks an important historical moment – early modern rural enclosure in England – when the contemporary hegemonic territorialization of property solidified. As an interaction device, territory helped reconstitute changing property relations, producing new social gradients premised on differential access and use of land. The 'property space' – naming, acting, talking, and bounding – changed as a result. In

DOI: 10.4324/9781003253389-3

particular, we can see increased importance put upon territorial exclusivity that centred individual rights, most particularly the right of the individual to exclude others. As such, the legal and practical defence of territory became of more pressing importance. As land becomes more sharply territorialized, commoners become deterritorialized. Legal doctrine – notably the very concept of 'property' itself – changed, as did imaginative and practical changes in 'space', particularly the practice of land surveying.

Let us begin by considering the changing concept of property itself. Property – particularly private property – was not given legal definition until relatively recently (Aylmer, 1980). This was not because people did not have a clear sense of the objects over which they exercised ownership. But this list was expansive. People would use 'property' to refer to 'one's name, spouse, children, parents, servants, friends, country, king, lord, body, soul, sins, debts, thoughts, death, and a lot of other possessive uses that stretch far beyond the legal pigeonhole that lawyers later labelled "property"' (Seipp, 1994, p. 32).

Legal historians tell us that from around 1290 to 1490, English lawyers did not have a term that had the scope and explanatory power that later lawyers found in the words 'property' or 'ownership': 'they lacked a word for legally protected interests in both land and goods, one that would assimilate these interests to some degree, and separate them from other legally protected relations' (Seipp, 1994, p. 31). Those designations that were available tended to be assigned to personal goods rather than land. This perhaps was because while goods and animals could be stolen or strayed, land stayed put. The identity of the rightful holder of land was common knowledge, while goods and animals required legal nametags via ascriptions of 'property' to some person.

The idea of private property as a form of absolute dominion was also conceptually unavailable. As Simpson (1986, pp. 88–89) notes, 'medieval lawyers never spoke of a person owning an estate in lands'. Rather, one thought of a person 'holding' land, this being measured by time: thus 'they hold the manor for an estate in fee tail, or for life, or whatever. . . . Nothing further need be said about anyone owning anything for the legal position to have been fully stated'. In earlier usage, '[o]ne did not say "this is my property", as we use the term now. Rather, one said "I have property in it" or "the property of it is to (or with) me"'. (Seipp, 1994, p. 33). The social relationality of property, obscured in its modern expression in the ownership model, was thus more fully evident. The interests that people had were, in principle at least, tied to interlocking feudal obligations of privilege and service.

Property relations were also highly localized in the manor, the basic unit of landholding following the Norman Conquest. Such relations were regulated by the local institution of the manor court, or court of survey. The court of survey recorded the conditions of the various local tenancies while also allowing for the collective governance of the common rights that existed within the manor. Over time, such practices became formalized as customary rights, notably the right of profit-à-prendre, or the right of taking something, and that of ease-ment – the right to habitation and movement on the land (Fields, 2017). Such rights served to buttress a strong sense of proprietorship realized in an embodied landscape of circulation and openness.

Collective or common property rights to manorial land were a vital resource, combining individual and collective rights to arable lands and 'waste' lands (uncultivated manorial land owned by the lord, such as meadows, woodlands, etc.). Arable land would be divided into strips or 'selions' in open fields that were then distributed to tenants to cultivate, the allocation, ploughing, and harvesting of which were collectively decided upon. Commoners also had the right to graze upon the waste, as well as harvest valuable resources from it (Neeson, 1993).

The result was a territorialization of property that departs markedly from the modern model:

> many persons other than the 'tenant in possession' would work and live on a given parcel of land, and derive benefit from it. Many others would take some of its produce, or simply make their way across it on the way to somewhere else. . . . The image of one individual owner, or even one family, excluding all others and taking all increase from a parcel of land would have been a vast oversimplification, and probably an unrecognizable image for holders of large or small parcels.
>
> (Seipp, 1994, pp. 45–46)

The value of landholding rested on its ordered inclusivity, not its exclusivity. Crucially, the primary relation of an individual to a parcel of land 'could be maintained without physically excluding others. Indeed, land had little value to the rightful holder if others were entirely excluded' (Seipp, 1994, p. 87). Even in the case of urban land, governed by forms of tenure that were less encumbered by feudal obligations, property was 'more conditional and less exclusive and individualistic than it is now. Contemporaries recognized the simultaneous existence of a plurality of interests in one space – some of them deferred, some contingent, and some barely enforceable' (Harding, 2002, p. 558).

While contemporaries 'were highly sensitive to spatial divisions and boundaries' (Harding, 2002, p. 552), their understandings did not necessarily parallel modern conceptions of trespass. If a single tenement 'belonged' to multiple parties, the occupier's rights to bar entry to others was often compromised: 'The right physically to enter a property figured largely in [legal disputes]: literally to bar the door to a legitimate claimant was to deprive or disseize him of a right and could lead to long litigation' (Harding, 2002, p. 555). Rather than the boundary being a bulwark against others, legal practice ensured that controls in the public interest were strongest at the interface between properties, the guiding principle being that 'the territorial integrity of the individual property was modified by increased obligations and restrictions at the margin' (Harding, 2002, p. 560)

Yet while it departed from the modern exclusive conception, territoriality was clearly present. English rural commons relied on multiple territorial rules, both external (think of the 'beating of the bounds') and internal (such that certain grazing areas may be off-limits to all commoners at particular times). The daily practices of commoning entailed spatial access and mobility, whether through designated footpaths or through a more general 'right to roam' across the Lord's land. The visual openness of the landscape bespoke a collective culture. Standing at the centre of the pre-modern village

> feels like standing at the hub of the whole system: the fields spread around you, the decision one with wheat, another with barley is written on the landscape. For all that individual men and women work their own bits of land, their economy is public and to a large degree still shared.
>
> (Neeson, 1993, p. 2)

Reterritorializing private property

While changes to English property can be traced to slow shifts over several centuries (Baker, 1971, pp. 121–175; Elden, 2013, pp. 213–241), it was in the early modern era that we begin to see a shift in the meaning of property in land. This entailed a slow, tentative, and contested movement in the property space, away from feudal entitlements, where land was held 'of' others, to a more recognizably modern conception of property as a basis for individualized entitlements to land that could be rented, used, sold, and willed (Overton, 1996). By the early seventeenth century, 'property' had been installed 'as a fundamental concept applying to land', from which it began to be possible to designate a single person as an 'owner' (Seipp, 1994, p. 80).

But this was a far from straightforward process (Sampson, 1990). Crucial was the role of the jurist St German, whose *Doctor and Student* in the 1520s was the first work on English common law in wide circulation to delineate a general law of property, applicable to land as well as goods, identifying an abstract and universal 'law of property' (*lex proprietatis*). St German refers to 'that generall lawe or generall custome of propretye wherby goods movable and unmovable be brought in to a certayne propretye so that every man may knowe his owne thinge' (quoted in Aylmer, 1980, p. 87). However, as Aylmer notes, St German failed to provide a definition of property itself. Only until 1607 did Cowell provide the first definition: 'Propertie signifieth the highest right that a man can have in anything; which is in no way depending on any other mans courtesie' (quoted in Aylmer, 1980, p. 89). However, Cowell immediately qualified this by noting that no one can have a property in their lands defined thus. Other than the Crown, all hold land mediately. Some later sixteenth-century definitions, moreover, applied the term only in relation to personal goods.

Edward Coke, the early seventeenth-century jurist, sharpened private property's teeth, distinguishing absolute property rights from 'qualified' or 'special' property rights, arguing that whoever held the 'absolute' property in a thing could assert their claim against the world, whereas they who held the 'special' interest could assert it against everyone but the 'absolute' owner. Later, lawyers began to make a stronger hierarchical distinction between the two. If the former was characterized as 'absolute', 'principal', 'true', or 'greater', the latter was 'qualified', 'conditional', 'mere', and 'a kind of' property (Seipp, 1994, p. 84). From this, a rule was emerging:

> whoever had the 'general' or 'absolute' property in a thing could assert that interest against everyone in the world, and whoever had the 'special' property could assert it against everyone but the 'general' or 'absolute' owner.
>
> (Seipp, 1994, p. 84)

The effect was significant. While multiple people could have different sorts or degrees of property interest in the same land, the lawyer's lexicon began to only allow for one 'owner', who was free to do with a thing as the law allowed.

Crucially, land itself also became an object capable of absolute ownership, fully entering the property space. As noted, in mediaeval England, it was goods and animals, not land, that came closest to a conception of absolute property. But from the sixteenth century onwards, English lawyers began to extend their model of ownership of goods and animals to landholding such that it was conceptually possible to imagine 'property in land' and 'owners of land'. Given the sharpening distinction between 'absolute' and 'special' property interests, noted previously, land began to be conceived of as a thing from which others were to be presumptively excluded, and the category of the 'owner' was figured as given particular privileges. The property space, in other words, began to be recalibrated via processes of 'naming' and 'acting':

> As land became more 'property-like', the newly named 'owner' acquired more freedom to alienate, to extract value in new ways, and to exclude others, while the long-recognized rights of other persons over the same land were diminished.
>
> (Seipp, 1994, p. 89)

The effect was to reconceptualize the social relationality of property 'Conflicts were no longer between holders of rights of common and "the lord of the manor" or "he who has the freehold". Now the protagonists were the commoner and the "owner of the soil" or "owner of the land"' (Seipp, 1994, p. 85).

It is hard to overestimate the importance of these conceptual changes to the concept of property in land and their contemporary reach. For my purposes, however, I wish to underscore the way in which property was reterritorialized. If, as noted previously, the premodern imaginary of a highly localized, relational geography of property was one of multiple persons accessing and using a given parcel of land, now lawyers increasingly invoked 'a stark mental image of one solitary person alone in complete and exclusive possession of one tract of land' (Seipp, 1994, p. 87).

To be in complete and exclusive possession required a reterritorialization of the modes of 'acting' within the property space. Take, for example, the action of trespass. For mediaeval lawyers, trespass was used to refer to many wrongs, from murder to diverting water onto someone's land (Seipp, 1996). While trespass to land was one of those wrongs, it would have been viewed in a different light. In particular, it would have been of less consequence, given the way in which land itself was routinely used and accessed by many. As such, only a limited set of 'entries' upon land were deemed a threat that deserved a remedy.

However, as property became understood in more singular, exclusive terms, the ancient action of trespass was applied specifically to defend landed property, now imagined in more sharply territorialized terms (Linklater, 2013, p. 37). McDonagh and Griffin (2016) point to a 'progressive spatialization' of the term so that 'the generalized medieval concept was increasingly used in early modern England to *discipline those who passed beyond a limit*' (my emphasis, 3). Edward Coke characterized traditional agrarian law as 'snares that might have lien heavy on the subject' (quoted in McRae, 1996, p. 163). As property is conceptually freed of such snares, it is re-imagined as a territory over which the owner should have an exclusive right. As such:

> the owner may retain to himself the sole use and occupation of his soil: every entry therefore thereon without the owner's leave . . . is a trespass or transgression.
>
> (Blackstone, 1768/1979b, p. 209)

These radical reworkings of the space of property were not exclusively the domain of the lawyer, however. Shifts in other practices and sites of expertise help to perform the reterritorialization of property into practice. Two in particular – surveying and husbandry – played a pivotal role.

Surveying and the revisualization of property space

Traditionally, as noted, the surveying of manorial lands was a practice undertaken at the 'court of survey'. Largely non-cartographic, this entailed an enumeration and valuation of assets and use-rights, with little emphasis given to the location or areal extent of lands (Beresford, 1998; Smail, 1999). It was conducted not by an outside expert but by a manorial official, with the help of those tenants whose memories went back the furthest (Taylor, 1947, p. 122). The traditional surveyor was required to 'butt and bound' the manor with the help of those tenants whose memories went back the furthest. This entailed walking around the land, recording the 'meeres, markes and boundes as have been very anciently used and accustomed', according to Fitzherbert's 1523 *Boke of Surveyeng* (Taylor, 1947, p. 122).

By the early seventeenth century, this form of 'performance cartography' (Woodward & Lewis, 1998, p. 4) began to give way to a new conception of surveying, now reframed as a technical endeavour, engaged in by experts in geometry, accurate measurement and cartography, the outcome of which was a map, drawn to scale (Blomley, 2014). While in 1500, maps were 'little understood or used', by 1600, 'they were familiar objects of everyday life'; '[t]he map as we understand it was effectively an invention of the sixteenth century' (Harvey, 1993, pp. 7–8). The old-fashioned surveyor, 'a man of classical education possessed of sound legal knowledge', was supplanted by the assistant 'whom he had been accustomed to term a "mere land-meater", employed to carry the measuring rod' (Taylor, 1947, p. 124). The survey was no longer a description of the use-rights that inhered in a particular site but a rendering of land as a bounded parcel of space. The survey, in other words, became spatialized as the concept of landed property 'as a bundle of assorted rights over different bits of territory gave way to the idea that property lay in definable pieces of soil' (Thompson, 1968, p. 10). The latter entailed a remarkable imaginative shift. So, for example, Love advises the surveyor to first imagine the manor as an abstract space, walking or riding around the manor once or twice so 'that you may have as it were a Map of it in your head' (1623/1687, p. 142). The next step is not to list property relations but to map property as bounded spaces. To do so requires that the entire manor be first rendered as a parcel of land. The surveyor is to delineate the entire manor, taking angles and length measurements, record all roads, lanes, and rivers, and then produce a map of the whole, which is to be filled in by surveying all the hedge lines of every field, redoing as necessary; surveying any additional fields that are not obviously bounded by a hedge, land, or river, and placing these relative to other fields; and finally producing a map of the whole, marking the location of the manor house as well as additional features such as woods and ponds.

If we assume, as we must, that mapping is performative rather than simply representational (Kitchin & Dodge, 2007), it becomes interesting to ask how emergent conceptions of surveying were implicated in changing conceptions of property's territoriality. Surveying produced the abstraction of 'space' itself. In so doing, the 'space' of property became imagined as actionable, in part due to the visual register in which it worked. These two points need unpacking. First, the modern survey may be said to assist in encouraging a view of property as a space rather than a bundle of localized relationships. Crucially, emergent forms of surveying relied heavily on a geometric conception of space. In so doing, space itself emerged in Western thought as something 'extensible and calculable, extended in three dimensions, and grounded on the geometric point' (Elden, 2005, p. 8). This is an important point. The surveyed map did not simply reposition property within a pre-existing spatial imaginary. In an important sense, it helped produce the very modern idea of space itself – and, by extension, a particular conception of territory – itself.

Geometry, in this sense, is more than an instrument for representation. As Elden (2005) notes, early moderns such as Descartes saw it as a site of calculation. Secondly, then, as geometry helped reduce space to a manipulable form, it became easier to conceive of property as a ter-ritorialized zone of action and calculation. As Sack (1983, p. 63) notes: 'to think of territory as emptiable and fillable is easier when a society possesses writing and especially a metrical geometry to represent space independently of events. . . . The coordinate system of the modern map is ideally suited'. Euclid's *Elements of Geometry* was first translated into English in 1570. In the preface, John Dee notes the connection between geometry and 'land-measuring' and praises '[t]he perfect sci-ence of Lines, Plaines, and Solides [which] (like a divine Justicier,) gave unto every man his owne' (quoted in McRae, 1993, p. 345). The early modern surveying manuals sought to educate and inculcate such a geometric sensibility, echoing the vigorous advocacy of mathemati-cal practitioners in related fields in sixteenth-century England, keen to demonstrate the utility of geometry and arithmetic to practical economic and political projects (Bennett, 1991; Johnston, 1991). The injunction, more generally, was to:

> reduce what you are trying to think about to the minimum required by its definition; visualize it on paper, or at least in your mind, be it the fluctuation of wool prices at the Champagne fairs or the course of Mars through the heavens, and divide it, either in fact or in imagination into quanta. Then you can measure it, that is, count the quanta.
>
> (Crosby, 1997, p. 228)

By counting the quanta, the survey made possible a view of land as that which could be differently appraised and evaluated. Surveyors (as well as kindred writers on husbandry, as we shall see) increasingly charac-terized the estate as an object of 'improvement' (that is, both an object of appropriation and a site for individual betterment), the effect of which was to reconstitute rights to land as something that could be:

> [c]learly and objectively . . . determined, in a manner which precludes competing or loosely held customary claims. Land

ownership is thus figured as reducible to facts and figures, a conception that inevitably undermines the matrix of duties and responsibilities that had previously been seen to define the manorial community. In the perception of the surveyor, the land is defined as property, as the landlord's 'own'.

(McRae, 1993, p. 341)

While the results of the court of survey were to be assessed and evaluated by members of the manorial community, the data generated by the modern survey were to be plugged into wider circuits of calculation,

THINGS
GOT PARTICULARLY
BUCK-WILD
WHEN THE PRACTISE OF
CARTESIAN MAPPING
EMERGED-

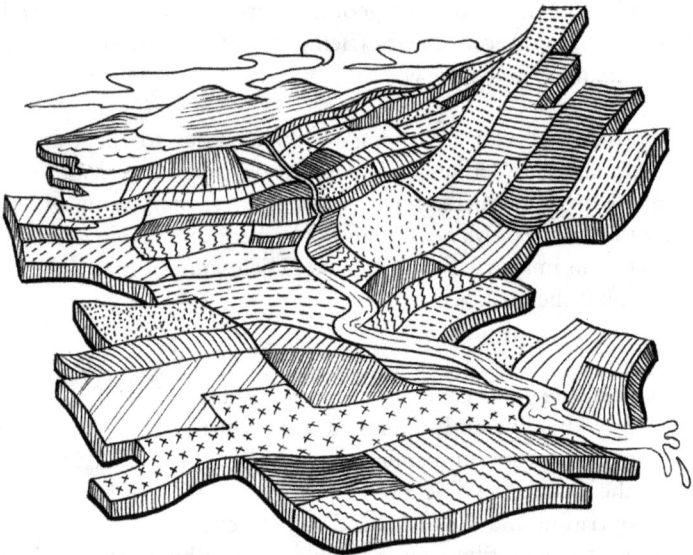

Figure 3.2 'Things got particularly buck wild. . .'.
Source: From sobelow.org; reproduced with permission.

appraisal, and comparison. For example, the modern surveyor insisted on the measurement of land through the use of universal metrics, such as the standard chain, tables of calculation, and instruments. Such metrological moves made possible a conception of the land as a resource which could begin to be plugged into wider circuits of comparison and economic calculation (Blomley, 2014).

Further, the modern survey worked in a different register. If the traditional surveyor relied on oral memory, the modern surveyor traded in visual objectivity. One of the practical qualities of the modern map, it was said, was that it promised to open up a space of clarity and certainty and 'retrieve and beat out all deacaied, concealed and hidden parcels [of land]' (Agas, quoted in McRae, 1993, p. 341). The surveyor participates in creating the world 'as exhibition', whereby space is set before the viewer (Mitchell, 1995). In Norden's *Surveyor's Dialogue*, a farmer queries why their lands needed to be portrayed on a map, asking, 'is not the field it selfe a goodly Map for the Lord to look upon?' Norden's surveyor replies that the map enables the Lord 'sitting in his chayre, [to] see what he hath, where and how it lyeth, and in whose use and occupation every particular is, upon the suddaine view' (Norden, 1618/1979, pp. 15–16). The advantage of the 'suddaine view' in allowing the landowner to 'know his own' reoccurs in surveying manuals, Delano-Smith and Kain (1999, p. 117) note. Now the Lord, 'sitting in his chayre at home, may justly knowe, how many miles his Manor is in circuite, and the circuit of any particular grounds, and wasts' (Worsop, quoted in Brückner & Poole, 2002, p. 624). Estate management increasingly became premised on the management of territory, best realized through visual surveillance and organization. Land became an object of distanced calculation, a departure from the more conservative tradition of estate management in which 'the best dung for the field is the master's foot' (McRae, 1993, p. 351, cf. Cosgrove, 1985). Initially referring to a parcel of land, the word 'plot' was increasingly used to refer to a map. The map, in other words, begins to become a substitute for the land itself, and 'a reduction of land and tenantry to their graphic and written representations takes on the status of truth' (Sullivan, 1994, p. 239).

Husbandry: doth not every man covet to have his alone?

The 'ingenious and active' landowner was the target not only of primers extolling modern forms of surveying. Husbandry manuals, offering practical advice on estate management, also became widespread in the late sixteenth and early seventeenth century, deploying a new rhetoric of improvement, productivity, and profit (McRae, 1996; Slack, 2015; Thirsk, 1983). To achieve these ends, it was argued, required that property relations be rearranged in a more exclusive and singular fashion. Manorial property was seen, too often, as deeply entangled and excessively relational, with multiple use-rights attached to the same parcel of land. Customary forms of tenure, including common right, were deemed an obstacle to 'improvement' (Thirsk, 1967). The freehold estate was thus to be preferred because it allowed the owner to make the most of what was now increasingly deemed to be his own (McRae, 1993).

It is for this reason that many of the husbandry manuals advocated forms of territorialized enclosure. Moore (1653, pp. 12–13) argued that waste could not be brought to productive use through the 'common husbandry' of the 'vulgar'. The only solution was the distribution of land to 'private owners, which being appropriated to their particular uses, will then be cleansed and purged of the former deformities, and so fully improved'. Is it better, Moore (1653) asks rhetorically, for you to

> have no particular property in [land] . . . [o]r to say *this is mine*, I can let, sell, or dispose it at my pleasure, and so assure me a certain means and estate (out of nothing) wherein others have not to do?
>
> (my emphasis)

Such a territorial strategy both reflects and inculcates an emergent logic of possessive individualism (Macpherson, 1962). 'Doth not every man covet to have his alone?' asks Moore rhetorically (1653, no page). Such a sensibility rests on a relation to land, now legally and, as noted previously, cartographically represented as a discrete territory. Blith (1652, p. 86) argues that when 'men know their own', 'improvement' will surely follow:

> Were every mans part proportioned out to himself, and laid severall [i.e., enclosed], it would so quicken and incline his spirits, that he would be greedy in searching out all opportunities of Improvement whatsoever the Land is capable of.
>
> (Blith, 1652, p. 86)

Put more bluntly, 'now that mens lands . . . is their owne, they may do with them what they list' (Standish, 1613, B1). For men to do 'what they list' on land that 'is their owne' requires a spatial reconceptualization of property. Property was imagined not just as a thing ('this is mine') but also as a territory from which others are to be excluded. Only then will 'improvement' follow. One striking example comes from Cressy Dymock's proposal for the 'division or setting out of land', designed to prevent the

> unremediable intanglements or intermixtures of interest of severall persons in the same Common, in the same field, in the same Close, nay sometimes in the same Acre. . . [and] the inconvenient passages made or allowed between divers grounds.
>
> (Hartlib, 1653, pp. 3–4)

Such 'intanglements' are now seen not as the interpersonal obligations and socialized property relations of manorial life but as the predatory incursions of those lurking 'outside' the boundary. Dymock worries at the poor who will let their pigs loose and 'on set purpose drive them thither by which means they will sometimes get a haunt of a piece of corn, and go into it so cunningly' (Hartlib, 1653, p. 7). The 'evill contrivance and inter-mixture of wayes and interests' (Hartlib, 1653, p. 8), Dymock fears, is the reason why many are unwilling to 'improve', for they 'have no place secure enough, but may every day one before the other expect, that the carelessness or wickedness of their Neighbours' may let in animals to 'destroy all their labours and charges in an instant'. Traditional property relations are thus reframed as impinging 'upon the farmer's sovereignty. . . [as] a form of theft' (McRae, 1996, p. 151).

For Dymock, the solution was to radically reterritorialize property through a remarkable set of geometric arrangements that severed the overlapping, relational ties of the commoning economy, placing the manor house at the centre of a series of enclosures (Figure 3.3). Both the subject (the owner) and the object (the land) are to be detached. For Dymock, such a plan fostered the separative self: 'here your house stands alone in the middle of all your little world' with your land, animals, and outhouses spread before you, ensuring a form of territorial purity, with 'no one ground to passe through into another, no probability of being trespassed upon by others . . . but the most perfect right and ample use of every foot of ground inclosed entire' (Hartlib, 1653, pp. 10–11). Such a panoptic territorial arrangement, allowing for efficient use, movement, and surveillance, was to be defended by a 'double hedge', with access only through a bridge or gate 'strong and stanch that I might let in what I would; but that nothing might get in without my leave' (Hartlib, 1653, p. 20).

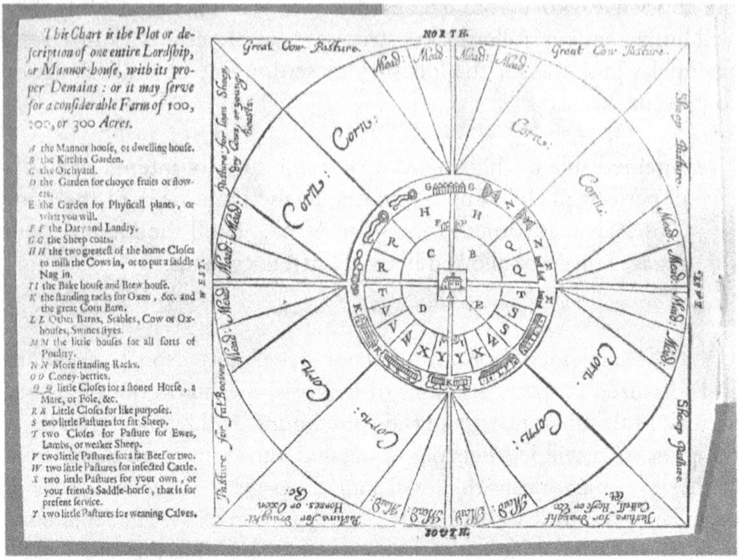

Figure 3.3 Dymock's 'little world'.

Source: From Hartlib, Samuel, 1653, The Huntington Library, San Marino, California, USA.

Dymock's reference to a hedge speaks to the enforcement of territory. Practically speaking, the expansion of enclosure required the imposition of new forms of spatial discipline and control. As the 'gatekeeping function' of the singular owner began to be foregrounded, so access to space had to be differently organized through forms of territorial communication and, crucially, enforcement, including the enrolment of territorial resources. For example, husbandry manuals encouraged the planting of thorn hedges along boundary lines. While hedges had long been used, they were to take on a different significance in this period, territorializing a new set of controversial conceptions of land and property rights. In so doing, the hedge aimed to prevent the forms of spatial movement associated with the commoning economy. This territorial discipline was socially directive: the body, notably that of the commoner and his or her beasts, became the site upon which new forms of discipline, materialized in the hedge, were to be realized.

The hedge aimed for two territorial purposes – communication and enforcement. Historically, the enclosure hedge had long communicated the creation of a 'close', a space of exclusive use and entitlement. Thus, 'the appearance of the enclosing hedge in the landscape served notice that henceforth the commodity of one individual was to preferred' (Manning, 1988, p. 25). This traditional semantic marker was mobilized on a larger scale to advance modern 'improvement'. The hedge also aimed to do practical work, enforcing an emergent form of class discipline through physically preventing territorial incursions. The improvement manuals of the day recommend the creation of the 'double hedges' that secured Dymock's geometric utopia. These were redoubtable defences, including ditches, that were to be 'plashed', or woven together, so as to be impenetrable to man or beast, using hawthorn, the organic barbed wire of the day.

Thomas Tusser's widely read husbandry manual, reportedly the biggest-selling book of poetry published during the reign of Elizabeth I (Bending & McRae, 2003, p. 124), encouraged the use of the hedge to enforce the new territories of property. Tusser extolled personal advancement, urging his reader to 'folow profit earnestlie' (1580/1873, p. 13). To do this, he repeatedly claimed, requires a stout, maintained hedge: 'Keepe safely and warely thine uttermost fence/with ope gap and breake hedge do seldome dispence' (1580/1873, p. 42). The hedge provides protection from the commoner, who now figures not as a holder of legitimate use-rights (to graze, glean, and so on) but as a predatory and threatening violator of the exclusive territorialized rights of the husbandman. Tusser harped on this theme in his eulogy to enclosure, which begins '[t]he countrie enclosed I praise,/the tother delighteth not me' (1580/1873, p. 140), frequently cited by later proponents of enclosure, such as Worlidge (1669, p. 11) and Blith (1652, pp. 87–92). 'More profit is quieter found', he concluded, 'where pastures in severall [enclosed] bee. . . [W]hat joie is it knowne/When men may be bold [confident, certain] of their owne!' (1580/1873, pp. 143–145). But for men to be 'bold' requires that that which is now 'their owne' be well guarded: 'keep safe thy fence', he counselled, 'scare breakhedge thence./A drab and a knave/will prowle to have' (1580/1873, p. 33).

The emergent property space clearly entails forms of representation or, as I described them earlier, 'talking'. Central to the process of enclosure was the denial of the legal subjecthood of the commoner and the validity of common right itself. As we see previous, these became reframed as 'intanglements' or trespasses. In his paean to enclosure,

Tusser (1580/1873, pp. 143–145) casts the commoner and their cow as a threat to the improved encloser, echoing contemporary home-owner's anxieties of the dispossessed urban poor at their gate:

The champion [commoner] robbeth by night,
And prowleth and filcheth by day:
Himselfe and his beast out of sight,
Both spoileth and maketh away
Not onely thy grasse, but thy corne,
Both after, and er it be shorne [the reference is to gleaning]. . . .
Pease bolt with thy pease he will have,
His household to feede and his hog:
Now stealeth he, now will he crave,
And now will he coosen and cog [cheat and defraud]. . . .
Laie [plan] never so well for to save it
By night or day he will have it.

Resisting reterritorialization

Now placed outside the hedge of enclosure, the commoner refused to accept her relegation and the denial of common right. The dispossessed commoner joins a long list of those who resist the exclusionary logics of capitalist and colonial property, simultaneously challenging its attendant territoriality. Predictably, those who sought to recover traditional geographies of access and use, denied by this form of 'bounding', often contested new forms of material territorialization. Thus, the enclosure hedge of the enterprising husbandman was a frequent target. Indeed, hedge-levelling, as it was known, became 'something of a national pastime' at the turn of the sixteenth century (Manning, 1988, p. 316). In 1596, for example, protestors in Oxfordshire called for a rising of the people 'to pulle downe the enclosures, whereby waies were stopped up, and arable lands inclosed, and to laie the same open againe' (Walter, 1985, p. 100).

Importantly, there are suggestions that for every organized protest, there were a dozen cases of people covertly 'throwing a gate off its hinges [or] uprooting some quicksets' (Thompson, 1993, p. 115). Such acts, of course, could be seen as a form of trespass. However, the opponents of enclosure often read the territory of property differently. The communicative messaging of territory, as noted previously, is far from transparent but is capable of alternative readings. For the commoner, the breaking of an enclosure carried a symbolism of its own (Blomley,

2007; Manning, 1988, p. 27). For the encloser, a hedge was a protective barrier; for the commoner, it was an illegitimate divider. For the former, the hedge materialized the private property owner's right to exclude. For the latter, it was an affront to the commoner's right not to be excluded (Blomley, 2016c). The breaking of a hedge, McDonagh and Griffin (2016) point out, was not simply directed at the boundary. It was also intended to open the space enclosed by the boundary in order to let the commoner's livestock in. Such enactments also served to 'perform' common right (McDonagh, 2013, p. 40), providing a physical means 'by which title and ownership could be inscribed on the land through use and daily practice' (McDonagh, 2009, p. 199).

In so doing, the commoner drew not only a deep-seated sense of customary property right but also an understanding of how property should be territorialized. Under the tradition of 'possessioning', for example, commoners sometimes claimed the right to tear down enclosures on commons or wastes during parish perambulations, carrying mattocks and axes for that purpose. Confronting the wholesale enclosures of 'improving' farmers, commoners continued this tradition, breaking or destroying hedges. As a marker of ownership, the hedge signalled an illegitimate encroachment upon common right. As such, to break it was not to break the law but to uphold customary right.

This period sees the early use of the terms 'leveler' and 'digger', later deployed in the revolutionary risings of the mid seventeenth century. To level a hedge signified the levelling of social distinction. In a remarkable document entitled 'The Diggers of Warwickshire to all other Diggers', a group of 'poor delvers and day labourers' issued a call to others to join the rising in condemnation of the 'devouring encroachers':

> We as members of the whole do feel the smart of these encroaching tyrants [i.e. enclosers], which would grind our flesh upon the whetstone of poverty . . . so that they may dwell by themselves in the midst of their herds of fat wethers [sheep].
>
> (Bending & McRae, 2003, p. 147)

The jab at the enclosers, who 'dwell by themselves', foreshadows the lines of the nineteenth-century peasant poet John Clare, who in 'The Mores' describes the 'owners little bounds. . . . In little parcels little minds to please/With men and flocks imprisoned ill at ease'.

By the mid seventeenth century, opponents of enclosure frequently used the hedge as a metaphor for the injustices of social division.

Winstanley's manifesto laments that '[t]he earth (which was made to be a common treasury of relief for all, both beasts and men) was hedged in to enclosures by the teachers and rulers, and the others were made servants and slaves' (quoted in Bending & McRae, 2003, p. 150). The enclosure of land 'hedges in some to be heires of Life, and hedges out others' (WInstanley, quoted in Manning, 1988, p. 30).

However, as such customary territorial enactments of property rights became reimagined as assaults on absolute property, so we see a hardening of exclusive territorialized property rights in land. The commoner's territorial affronts, including the 'depasturing' of animals (i.e., grazing commoner's animals on enclosed land), were thus often aggressively punished. By 1600, hedge breakers at Ingatestone, Essex, were to be whipped until they 'bleed well' (Rackham, 1986, p. 190).

Yet the record also reveals that the practice of commoning was not so easily suppressed: 'It would take many years, if it happened at all, before [the] idea of right . . . was worn down into a privilege, and before commoners would accept that privileges could be taken away' (Neeson, 1993, p. 163). One striking example is the practice of gleaning, the custom that permitted poor cottagers (traditionally women) to enter onto harvested land to collect leftover grain. An important source of food and income for labouring families, gleaners faced increasing difficulties as farmers began to seek legal sanctions in order to limit access. Custom thus became crime. For example, an action for trespass was brought against Mary Houghton for gleaning in closes at Timworth in Suffolk. At the Court of Common Pleas in 1788, Lord Loughborough rejected her defence on the grounds of common right, arguing that 'the nature of property . . . imports exclusive enjoyment' (quoted in Thompson, 1993, p. 139). Mr. Justice Wilson concurred:

> No right can exist at common law, unless both the subject of it, and they who claim it, are certain. In this case, both are uncertain. . . . The soil is his [the farmer's], the seed is his, and in natural justice his also are the profits.
>
> (Thompson, 1993, p. 140)

As Thompson notes: 'how could enjoyment be exclusive if it did not command the power to exclude from property's physical space the insolent lower orders?' (1993, p. 139).

If new habits of territory were in the making, they were not, however, universally taken up by the 'lower orders'. King (1989) notes that gleaning continued, despite the attempt of landowners to publicize the decision

> Eleven years after the [1788] judgment one of the largest farmers in Easthorpe, north Essex, challenged a woman gleaning in his fields and 'desired her not to glean any longer'. She refused to comply, answering simply that 'it was not his property but belonged to her'. When he returned next morning he found 'she had brought upwards of thirty other persons with her' who were quietly asserting that the gleanings were their property too.
>
> (120)

Moreover, the legal attacks mounted against gleaners in the eighteenth and nineteenth centuries were often unsuccessful. Indeed, in one case, a farmer who seized a gleaner's bag was charged with theft. Gleaners acted collectively to defend what they regarded as their right, often successfully arguing that they enjoyed local customary rights. So even though courts tended to find for the farmers, 'the continued strength of the gleaner's rights in practice largely prevented the actualization of Lord Loughborough's absolute conception of property rights' (King, 1989, p. 147; Shakesheff, 2002).

Yet the more sharply territorialized conception of private property was clearly on the ascendant. It was sustained, in large part, by a set of claims regarding ownership and personhood 'wherein the latter was defined through and on the basis of one's capacity to appropriate' (Bhandar, 2018, p. 4). Locke, famously, made clear that the capacity to appropriate resided only in the 'Industrious and Rational' – that is, rich, white men (Locke, 1980/1690). Ownership, therefore, was clearly inflected with a racialized and colonial logic:

> by the 1600s, improvement writers were assigning [waste] the perjorative meaning of land that was empty: terra nullius. If the common landscape was empty, its copyhold users were recast in much the same way, as the inhabitants of empty landscapes – as was by now occurring in other parts of the British overseas empire. Much like the Amerindians of North America, commoners were recast as 'savages'.
>
> (Fields, 2017, p. 54)

Eighteenth-century Scottish 'improvers' likened Scottish Highlanders to Africans and Indigenous Americans (Ross, 2011), while the violent dispossession of the Irish was rationalized by English assumptions of their paganism and thus barbarian status (Canny, 1973). Those who thought the English too severe in their dispossessive acts were reminded by one apologist that the Irish preferred to 'live like beastes, voide of lawe and all good order', and they were 'more uncivill, more uncleanly, more barbarous and more brutish in their customs and demeanures, then in any other part of the world that is known'. (Canny, 1973, p. 588). Gilbert, Raleigh, and Frobisher, who had experience in Irish colonialism, had little difficulty in applying the same dispossessive, racialized logic in their violent encounters with the Indigenous peoples of the 'New World' (Canny, 1973, p. 596, Bhandar, 2018, pp. 39–47). To understand the particular convergence of territory and property, we cannot only turn to European rural enclosure. Racialized colonial encounters and their continued afterlife also play a crucial role in forming property's territoriality.

4

Racializing territory[1]

Precisely because property's territory has become doxic, it is useful to look at spaces or moments in which such arrangements are made more visible. To do so, one useful strategy is to learn from those who are forced to confront and negotiate dominant territorial property rules – this I explore in more detail in Chapter 6. It is also useful to focus on moments of radical change when relations to land are remade. As noted, the enclosure of common lands in the seventeenth century is one moment. For now, however, let me offer a different but surely related moment: the dispossession of Indigenous land in early twentieth-century British Columbia, Canada. The example I give draws from testimony given at a joint federal and provincial commission charged with addressing the 'Indian land question' between 1913 and 1916.[2] In 1914, the commissioners travelled to Kwakwaka'wakw territory in what is now the northern tip of Vancouver Island and surrounding lands. Kwakwaka'wakw people have occupied this land since time immemorial, grounded in complex systems of law, governance, and culture (Powell & Webster, 1994).

All the dimensions of property's territoriality – the imaginaries, production, violent enforcement, experience, and contestation – are evident in the testimony. My focus here is on settler enactments of territory and property as experienced by the Kwakwaka'wakw people themselves and as rationalized and sustained by the commissioners.

1 This chapter has benefitted from ongoing conversations with and advice from fellow members of the Decommission Collective (Sarah Hunt, Mayana Slobadian, Marianne Nicholson, Paige Raibmon, and Brenna Bhandar).
2 The Royal Commission on Indian Affairs for the Province of British Columbia (also known as the McKenna-Mcbride Commission) – testimony at http://ourhomesarebleeding.ubcic.bc.ca. Copy with author.

DOI: 10.4324/9781003253389-4

Of course, we can only get an imperfect sense of this contact zone, given the profound constraints both of the colonial archive (unusually, testimony was recorded verbatim, although usually translated) and the highly limited terms of reference of the commission itself (discussions of 'Indian title', for example, were off-limits). There are many loud silences and absences in the testimony. It is also worth noting that testimony almost always comes from men. As a result, Indigenous women's relationship to land and water is often obscured or downplayed. Indigenous resistance, past and present, is only touched on here, given the power relations at work in the commission. This is a topic I return to in the final chapter.

Colonial settlement entails the simultaneous remaking of property and space, practically and ideologically reworking relations between land and people. Predicated on racialized notions of the human, property's territoriality was, and continues to be, weaponized by settlers. Settler territory, I demonstrate, becomes an instrument of violence and spatialized surveillance, opening up propertied space to settlers while confining space and possibility to Indigenous people. White territories became inviolable and non-negotiable, while Indigenous territoriality became remade as contingent and permeable. Yet such radical remakings are justified as equitable and beneficial.

Property, it has been convincingly argued, relies upon and helps sustain whiteness (Harris, 1993; Inwood & Bonds, 2017). The evolution of property law has been articulated through the attribution of value to the lives of those defined as having the capacity, will, and technology to appropriate, racializing those deemed unfit to own property. The justification for property ownership is thus bound to a highly racialized concept of the human, reliant on a 'process of racial sorting that creates a racial hierarchy while at the same time marking some as unworthy of life' (Dorries, 2022, p. 310). The social powers that property's territorialization accord are also embedded in such racial logics. Territoriality, Wolfe (2006, p. 389) reminds us, 'is settler colonialism's specific, irreducible element'.

Similarly, by the time of the commission, a relatively liberal provincial policy had given way to the assertion that Indigenous people had never owned land, thus rendering extinguishment irrelevant. This 'white myth' declared 'that British Columbia had been in essence an empty land, devoid of society, government, or laws. . . . [A]ll land in the colony was not only under British sovereignty but also directly owned by the Crown' (Tennant, 1990, pp. 40–41). This drew from notions that paired civilization with forms of cultivation legible to settlers. The resultant 'racial regime of ownership that interpellated Indigenous populations as lacking the requisite attachment to land and practices of cultivation to be owners of their land' (Bhandar, 2018, p. 50) continues to frame the colonial encounter in British Columbia. The absence of individualized property claims on the landscape that accorded with Western territorial logics combined with racialized assumptions regarding the lack of capacity for abstract thought into a dispossessive tautology:

> the alleged lack of mental capacity for abstract thought explains the absence of legible forms of ownership, and the apparent absence of ownership justifies the conclusion that these racial subjects lack the capacity for abstract thought.
>
> (Bhandar, 2018, p. 58)

Consequently, Indigenous people's claims to land were deemed both an impossibility, and an impediment, as Joseph Trutch, Commissioner for Lands and Works in British Columbia, made clear in 1867:

> The Indians regard these extensive tracts of land as their individual property but of by far the greater portion thereof they make no use whatever, and are not likely to do so; and thus the land, much of which is either rich pasture, or available for cultivation and greatly desired for immediate settlement, remains in an unproductive condition, is of no real value to the Indians, and utterly unprofitable to the public interests.[3]

By the time of the commission, such conceptions were overlain with assumptions regarding the inevitable disappearance of Indigenous peoples and arguments that Indigenous land tenure and governance were impediments to their 'civilization'.

The exploration of colonial contact zones, like Vancouver Island, allows us to see the manner in which colonialism is 'enacted locally, on the ground' (Harris, 2020, p. 176; Wolfe, 2016). Most immediately, testimony before the commission offers us a window into the violent colonial remaking of property relations on the ground, or what Raibmon (2008) terms the 'microtechniques of dispossession'. The remaking of property entailed the making of settler territory,

---

3 Trutch, Joseph 1867: 'Lower Fraser River Indian Reserves' Papers connected to the Indian land question 1850–1875, page 202. https://open.library.ubc.ca/viewer/bcsessional/1.0060734#p37z-3r0f: (last accessed 25 December 2021)

and the concomitant deterritorialization of Indigenous land relations, via the racialized denial of Indigenous relations to land and
the privileging of settler law. Settler land policy imagines Indigenous territory as socially emptiable space to be filled with Western
notions of boundary and property. As is evident in the testimony,
the installation of this racial regime of ownership (Bhandar, 2018)
inaugurated new territorial exclusions that made Kwakwak'wakw
life impossible.

Territorial containment

One pervasive thread to the testimony is a characterization of pervasive spatial confinement, of 'a world without spaciousness' (Fanon,
1963, p. 39). As an Indigenous leader in the neighbouring West Coast
Agency put it, '*It is just as if we are in a tub – we can't go anywhere without
bumping into whitemen*' (p 5, my emphasis). Alf Lageuse of the Nimpk-
ish Band (now the 'Namgis First Nation') noted that his village was
'guarded on this side and on that side with foreigners' (p 137). Chief
George Poleetami lamented the loss of the land 'owned by my forefathers' and complained that the reserves 'measured out for us' are too
small: 'there is hardly room to turn around in them' (66).

The most immediate effect of being 'in a tub' is that Kwakwaka'wakw
can no longer access places they were used to, a powerful expression
of the bounding work of the settler property space. This sense of spatial containment, realized through the imposition of alien territoriality and the associated denial of Indigenous governance and law, is
powerfully evidenced in the testimony of Tsukaite, one of the chiefs
of the Nackwacto Tribe (now Gwa'sala-'Nakwaxda'xw Nations) from
Blunden Harbour:

> I ask for the return of my country to me, and that the reserves be
> no more . . . What has been done to me with my country would
> be the other way – I would have measured pieces off for the
> whiteman instead of the whitemen measuring off pieces for me.
>
> (243)

Using similar corporeal imagery, Chief Lagis sought 'to put forth my
hand to pull some of [my land] back as it looks like as if the Government wants it wrenched out of our hands' (170).

This sense of spatial containment, of being 'guarded' on every side by settlers, is territorially manifested in the inability to access spaces previously available for hunting, fishing, and gathering, echoing Cole Harris' characterization of the everyday enforcement of settler property. Given the thin reach of the colonial state, he argues, it was settler landowners who enforced colonial property rights, monitoring Indigenous movements: 'Such watching, backed by the law, turned Native people into trespassers. It defined where they could and could not go. . . . [T]he management of movement associated with property rights was the most essential discipline imposed upon them' (2003, p. 271).

Frequently this 'management of movement' is referenced in the testimony. Chief Owahagaleese of the Kwawkwelth Band (now the Kwakiutl First Nation) complained that 'we have no place to log. Everywhere the land is called "Claims" and we cannot touch them. If we cut a tree off them we would get into trouble' (p. 109). Land is carved up into discrete territories over which exclusive settler property claims are now operative. Chief Tsukaite notes that the arrival of the commissioners marked the moment when he came to know 'that I have no country which I thought belonged to me'. To cross the line is to invite legal violence, whether formalized or extra-legal. 'When my children tries to cut some trees down', he notes, 'they are threatened and put in jail in the places where I thought belonged to me' (243).

If accessing land for timber, canoes, logs or firewood, or hunting is compromised by settler territoriality, then access to the fishery is even more controversial, judging by the testimony. Fishing has been 'taken by the whitemen who is coming here now' (39). Fishing places are fast disappearing: 'we feel that we have not got much of that even left – It is getting less and less every year' (91). Fish traps and fish netting are no longer permitted. Judging by the testimony, criminalization is objectionable as it violates Indigenous law and territoriality. Chief Tlageglass of the Kwawainuck Band (now the Gwawa̱'enux̱w First Nation) criticized those who come 'and fish on my rivers. . . . It is not only just now that I want to get my places, it has always been mine. I have marks there by which I know that it belongs to me from a long time ago' (228). Interestingly, the response of informants was often a demand for territorial powers, seeking exclusive rights to access resources, presumably echoing pre-existent forms of territorial regulation: 'We ask for powers to enable us to stop the white men' (198). Chief Owahagaleese of the Kwawkwelth Band (now the Kwakiutl First Nation) explained that such an 'exclusive right to these places where we get our food' (98–99) would return valued rights and freedoms.

(Re)learning territory

Powers 'to stop the white men' are not available, of course. Rather, it is the powers of the whitemen that must be reckoned with. The commissioners constantly feel obliged to train Indigenous people on the new territorialized rules, predicated on concepts such as trespass, whereby merely entering land that is held by another or taking resources that belong to a setller, even if useless is not allowed. Property's territoriality must be reimagined, with new communicative codes signalled. Commissioner McKenna notes that while 'Indians are free to hunt the same as whitemen on all lands that are not fenced in', if a 'whiteman has fenced his land, or if he has any natural boundaries showing his land, then you have no right to hunt and trap upon that land without the consent of the owner' (33). Whiteman's fences must be learned and respected. Even going on to another person's land to 'cut the dead trees that would be useless to the whiteman' is forbidden. To cross the line, regardless of intent or action, is to violate the sanctity of territorialized private property and the imagined mutual security that it gives to all:

> We cannot give you any privileges to cut down trees off the Reserve because they may belong to some white man or the Government; in the same way that the Indians would not want anyone to come and cut wood on their Reserves, and naturally whitemen would not like Indians to do the same on their land.
>
> (3)

However, if the territoriality of settler property is obvious to the commissioners it is far from clear to Kwakwaka'wakw witnesses. They describe, for example, how they are only now encountering settler maps, demarcating reserve land. 'Our forefathers were never asked about' the reserves marked on maps, complains Chief Cosahollis, 'and we have never heard anything about them, and that is the reason we refuse to accept them' (90). Chief Laguese notes that it is only with the arrival of the commission that:

> our eyes have been opened . . . You ought to have seen us in the general meeting this morning before you came – We had the plans, and one would say (referring to the Indian Reserves on the plans) 'where is it' 'whose is it' and we cannot tell you. We want to show you how helpless we are, and we think the Indian Agent should have told us about all these things.
>
> (89)

The meaning of spatial metrics like the acre are also unclear. 'We don't know how much an acre is', responds an informant. We 'just named it that because we heard the whitemen naming it' (9). Yet as noted Indigenous territoriality is apparently ignored or effaced by settlers. Chief Humseet asks that 'the marks that are [on his land] to be taken off that place. There are posts there. I want them to be pulled up for I have a mark there myself; all the Indians have a mark there' (183).

The legal concept of reserve land is unclear, moreover. What is its meaning, asks Johnnie Ferrie? Is it only a loan? It means that it is held in trust for the Indians, who can use and occupy it, is the reply. 'Does that mean that the land does not belong to the Indians?' he asks. The commissioner dodges the uncomfortable reality that it does not, emphasizing that it cannot be used by anyone other than Indians. No whiteman can touch it, trespass on it, or interfere with it in any way whatsoever: 'The Government prevents that and stands between the white man and the Indian and protects them on their reserves'. 'We don't like the name "Indian Reserve"', Johnnie Ferrie responds, 'we would like it to be named "Indian lands"' (252–253).

It is important to contextualize these apparent confusions. It is too easy to see them as simply the response to the imposition of an alien system of land governance and spatial metrics or to assume that a simpler system, absent property rules, was confronting a more sophisticated land tenure system with multiple forms of ownership, including fee simple private property, leases, and state property. Indigenous informants are not only grappling with a new system and its associated territorial rules but also confronting the organized erasure of a complex and highly organized system of Kwakwaka'wakw land tenure and governance. While epistemologically different from settler property, this cannot be reduced to simplistic and racist settler imaginaries of the 'noble savage', living in a world beyond property. Thus the questions asked of the commission: Why do your laws hold? Why can't we access that which has always been ours? Why don't we own the land that has been reserved for us? These are not naïve questions but entirely reasonable, grounded in the legal geographies of Indigenous law and sovereignty. As Mayana Slobadian points out, 'these chiefs really were *qualified interrogators*, not just unacquainted or inexperienced. It's not that it didn't make sense to them – it doesn't make sense, period. They were constantly pointing that out back then, and it's us that's just starting to understand'.[4]

---

4 My sincere thanks to Mayana Slobadian not only for this comment but also for her broader insights on the Kwakwaka'wakw testimony.

Communicating territory

So it is also important to turn our attention back to the commissioners and the manner in which they respond to these crucial questions.
Such questions often strike at the taken-for-grantedness not only of
settler sovereignty but also of the territoriality of settler property itself.
In so doing, such notionally simple questions open up the contradictions that course through settler territoriality, with its differential racial
calculus. So, for example, the exclusions of settler territory are justified by the claim that if certain land is no longer available, so reserves
are exclusive to Indians. As Commissioner Macdowall noted: 'Indian
Reserves are guarded in the same way as the property of a whiteman,
and no whiteman is allowed to trespass on an Indian Reserve. In fact, it
covers a greater penalty than for trespassing on whiteman's land' (151).
If whiteman's land is off limits to you, Indigenous people are reminded,
then reserve land is off limits to them. This common refrain – which
obviously ignores the massive inequality of land (re)allocation and the
fact that reserve land is not owned by the Nation – is curious. At one
level, perhaps, it suggests a desperate attempt by the commissioners
to skate over the brutal realities of colonial dispossession. At another,
perhaps, it enacts an old settler story that yokes territorialized private property to settlement, security, and resolution. Locke's treatise
on property traces the move from the simpler world of those who
'wandered with their flocks, and their herds . . . freely up and down'
(1980/1690, p. 37) to the sharply bounded territories of individualized
title. With civilization and advancement, goes the story, so people:

> settled themselves together. . ., and then, by consent, they came in
> time, to set out the bounds of their distinct territories, and agree
> on limits between them and their neighbours; and by laws within
> themselves, settled the properties of those of the same society. . .,
> and thus . . . we see how labour could make men distinct titles to
> several parcels of it, for their private uses; wherein there could be
> no doubt of right, no room for quarrel.
>
> (Locke, 1980/1690, pp. 38, 39)

As the presumptively wandering 'Indian' reconciles themselves to the
newly inscribed distinct titles and several parcels of the whiteman and
the 'Indian', so too can they embrace the benefits of security and certainty that supposedly comes with territorialized property. The 'savage',
without property, must live in poverty. Only with civilized property

can men enjoy the 'established expectation' that comes with the protection of the laws, equitably ensuring both the 'happiness of the cottage' and the 'security of the palace' alike (Bentham, 1999/1830, p. 53). Yet the territorial realities on the ground belie the optimistic Lockean geographies of 'distinct territories' generating settlement and harmony. For if settler land is off limits, then it is clear from the testimony that reserve land is far from exclusive. Timber on reserve land appears to be routinely cut down by settlers. Why don't you make more canoes, Chief George Pokleetami of the Nahkwockte Band was asked? 'Because the whitemen that have come around here won't let us. They threaten us if we cut the cedar down for our canoes'. Do you not have cedar on your own reserve? No, '[w]hite men cut down all our cedars and we have no cedar left for our canoes' (83). Settlers' livestock graze on reserve garden plots (p 150). Creeks on reserves are diverted or damned by canneries (p 152). Phone wires are run through reserve land (p 158). When alerted to these encroachments, the commissioners note that such actions may be unlawful (as indeed they are) and advise complainants to contact the relevant authorities (who are unlikely to be sympathetic) before counselling Indigenous people in the workings of settler legal territoriality, and the need to conform to it (put fences around your livestock, don't cross into settler territory without permission, and so on).

Territorial boundaries, then, are differentially racialized, becoming either permeable or hardened, depending on assigned status. Indigenous traditional territory becomes open to Crown and settler incursion. The whiteness of property is such that 'only particular forms of possession – those that [are] characteristic of white settlement – [are] recognized and legitimated' (Harris, 1993, p. 1722). Settlers access land reserved for 'Indians' with impunity, while land stolen by settlers is unavailable to Kwakwaka'wakw people. Yet, again and again, this territorialized differential is presented by the commissioners as horizontal, benefitting both 'Indians' and 'whitemen'.

So in a meeting with the Koskemo Band (now the Quatsino First Nation), for example, Kutesh asks whether it is permissible to cut trees off-reserve. The commissioners tell Kutesh that this is impossible, as off-reserve trees

> may belong to some white man or the Government; in the same way that the Indians would not want anyone to come and cut wood on their Reserves, and naturally whitemen would not like Indians to do the same on their land.

(3)

What about cutting dead trees for drying fish that would be useless to the owner? No, is the response: 'You can't go on other peoples' land without the owner giving you permission to do so'. Whitemen's boundaries are sacrosanct. Similarly, as asserted, a reserve

> cannot be used for anything else but for the Indians. No white man can touch it, trespass on it, or interfere with it in any way whatsoever. The Government prevents that and stands between the white man and the Indian and protects them on their reserves.
>
> (252–253)

Such territorial remakings and the associated property space rework relations between people, granting rights to settlers, and enforcing duties on Indigenous people. They rest on a racial calculus that privileges settler relations to land at the same time as devaluing Indigenous land relations. Yet the politics of property is often sanitized through forms of displacement. Power is depersonalized via 'papers from Ottawa' or threats of gaol. Power is also seemingly enforced by territory itself rather than the will of the owner. Harry Tlakwackalas of the Quatsino Band (now the Quatsino First Nation) asks where he and his people can hunt. Commissioner McKenna responds that Indians are free to hunt on unfenced land. However: 'if a whiteman has fenced his land, or if he has any natural boundaries showing his land, then you have no right to hunt and trap upon that land without the consent of the owner' (34). Communicative territorial acts, such as fencing, serve as regulators, in other words. The interpersonal relations central to property are displaced to the fence or boundary.

Enforcing territory

Settler's territorial powers are clearly enforced in violent ways. Such violences are generalized. That territory can be, literally, a land of fear is widespread in the testimony. Indeed, the immanent possibility of settler violence is often sufficient to enforce settler territoriality:

> Whenever we try to catch the salmon that run in our river, we are afraid to take them because of the threats that are made to us by the whitemen.
>
> (247).

Such violences surely reflect racist animus and the 'defensive paranoia' tied to property's territoriality (Hayes, 2020, p. 327). Land, unlike many other assets, is hard to surveil. The boundary thus becomes a simultaneous space of security and anxiety. Settler violence also speak to the boundary work of territoriality in this emergent contact zone and the associated work of racialization that is performed 'when colonizers are threatened with the requirement to share social space with the colonized' (Wolfe, 2016, p. 14).

Yet while physical assaults on Indigenous 'trespassers' may, technically, be a violation of private law powers, we also need to recognize that settler territorial performances cannot be divorced from colonial law. One common Indigenous complaint, for example, relates to the occupation or destruction of Indigenous buildings by settlers. So seemingly routine is this that examples often appear in passing during routine testimony when Indigenous witnesses report on the characteristics of particular parcels of land:

[T]here was a house there but the whiteman destroyed it. . . . [H]e told us to take the house away, but before we could do so he destroyed it.

(4)

Number 4 Reserve contains six houses, but one was destroyed by a whiteman camping there, who used the house for firewood. A woman was ordered out of her own house by a whiteman at gun point. The Indian Agent was advised, but 'he never paid any attention to it' (177).

It is too easy to characterize these violent dispossessive acts simply as aberrations from settler law. For in a very real sense, this *is* settler law. These routine expressions of settler violence manifest pre-emption practices that empower settlers to occupy 'Crown land' and, after a period of time, and the performance of certain practices, acquire title. Formally speaking, pre-emption claims by settlers are supposed to avoid reserves and 'Indian settlements'. However, the absence of formal policing on the ground, a generalized indifference or racist hostility to Indigenous people, provincial opposition to Indian title, the cultural and legal obligation to 'improve' a bounded and defensible space, the lack of a requirement for an initial survey, and a deliberately relaxed set of criteria for pre-emptions ('Indian settlements', notably, were never defined) combine to incentivize settlers to forcibly establish territorial 'facts on the ground' by clearing Indigenous territorial markers, legible to settlers, such as houses. With the visible markers of settlement excised, the land becomes free for pre-emption by these 'imperial precursors' (Blackhawk, 2006). When the whitemen 'come to my places, they come and break into my houses and burn the boards up', laments Chief Tlageglass. 'The house of my son was burned down by whitemen; that is another thing that pains my heart' (228). Whitemen break in to our houses and use the boards for firewood. They take our canoes, and steal our traps, the chief notes (221). This territorial vigilantism must be viewed not as an *exception* to state practice, in other words, but as a logical *extension* of it (Gazit, 2015).

It is not just physical settlements that become targets for settlers. Land already cleared by Indigenous people also becomes frequently seized. Chief Owahagaleese notes that land at a place called Tsikwkwyn that used to be a village has been seized: 'the whitemen came along and seeing the place cleared they put their house up there and stayed there' (97). Land seizure occurs even with clear territorial markers of an Indigenous presence. We see this process in the powerful testimony of Chief Cesaholis of the Tsah-waw-tineuch (now Dzawada̱'enux̱w First Nation), in a telling example of the erasure and marginalization of Indigenous women's property and associated legal geographies. A settler called McKay pre-empted a parcel of land, presumably attracted by its fertility and openness. However, this was no 'emptiable space' but an estuarine garden, 'the place where the women used to take the roots out of the ground', over which Indigenous territoriality was at work: 'we know it to this day they used to have a mark on it; individual marks for each one of them. They put down stakes the mark the boundary lines for each one of them'. However, these markers were either invisible to McKay or, more likely, simply ignored: 'to our surprise this whiteman came and just took the place and never asked us anything about it and our women were surprised to be ordered away from that place and they don't know why they were ordered away when they go there to get food'. McKay destroyed the baskets and digging tools of the women and 'immediately put a fence around the place enclosing the place where our women used to get the food, and for the first time then we come to know the troubles that we are in now in our own land' (207–208).

Depoliticizing territory

While Indigenous houses and gardens are, if anything, targets for settler seizure, whitemen's territory is inviolable. Settler property becomes 'facts on the ground', unavailable for conversation or dispute, even if those claims are clearly in violation of settler law, or title has yet to be finalized, as in the case of pre-emption claims, or is merely a lease. Take this conversation, in which Quocksistala (p. 31) requests a 'small place' next to a 'small river'. Commissioner McKenna responds:

> That land is owned by a whiteman and you cannot get that land – it belongs to Leeson's father. We cannot do anything for you in regard to that place. *We cannot give you land that is already owned by a whiteman.*
>
> (my emphasis)

Quocksistala responds by noting that 'we know that before the white man came that we owned that part of the country', and then asks, 'since you have told me that it belongs to a whiteman now, do we understand that the Government has deprived us of the land and our food?' (32). McKenna reiterates his claim that whiteman's land is unavailable: 'That land has been given to the white-man by the Government and it cannot be taken away from him'. The absurdity of 'taking away' whiteman's land is patently obvious to McKenna as he continues: 'You might as well go and claim the cannery' (32).

Land becomes property, Saito (2015, p. 50) notes, 'when lived on by some people, but not by others. Without whiteness, it is not property'. Yet as is clear, such doxic certainties are powerfully challenged in the commission hearings. Quocksistala's rejoinder to McKenna's dismissive claim is a blunt, powerful question: 'Do I understand that because the whiteman's house is there that that is the reason we cannot get it?' McKenna's answers, in effect, in the affirmative: 'The man . . . got it from the Crown and we cannot do anything with it' (32).

Clearly, this rests on the assumption that settler law trumps Indigenous law. But it may also turn on the reifying work of territorialization. Assertions of settler privilege become transformed into bounded, objective territories. Claims become parcels. White desire becomes a fence, and a map. As McKenna notes, the man 'got it' and thus 'we cannot do anything with it'. Settlers acquire 'land', it appears, rather than a racialized social allocation of legally sanctioned exclusionary power. As property becomes a spatialized, and hence objectified, 'fact', so it becomes depoliticized.

Moreover, the commissioners attempt to depoliticize dispossession and theft through an appeal to sovereignty. A settler's land claim is non-negotiable because he has received title from the state – he 'got it from the Crown'. In a similar exchange at Alert Bay, Mahmalillikullah (now

Mamalilikulla First Nation) Chief Negai objects to the timber leases
that have been allocated on his land:

> The country does not belong to the Government, and they have no
> business to sell it. What business has anyone to go and sell that land
> without asking if I had no more use for it[?] What right have they got
> to sell it before I was through with it because I was the owner of it[?]
> (132)

The commissioners responded by noting that the state has sold the
land legally, and it is not for us to question that: '*The Government is
over us as well as over you*, and therefore we have no right to question
what they have done. They have claimed the land and granted it, and
therefore we cannot meddle with that' (132–133, my emphasis). Like
Indian land claims, settler land claims are off the table. Sovereign power
is 'over us' all, supposedly protecting us all.

To the extent that sovereignty is 'over us', it is not 'before us' and
thus unavailable for discussion. To question it is absurd. You might
as well 'go and claim the cannery' (32). Yet sovereign territoriality is
clearly 'before' Kwakwaka'wakw witnesses and continues to be ques-
tioned. This becomes clearer in the many discussions of land that has
clearly been granted to settlers in violation of settler law or land that is
illegally claimed under a pre-emption, for which the Crown grant has
not yet been granted.

Yet such expressions of territorial vigilantism are also, it seems, non-
negotiable. In the neighbouring West Coast Agency, for example, a
complaint is made that an Indigenous man returned to his house (on
land 'cleared by the Indians a long time ago' – p 106) to find a 'whiteman living in his house, and this man told him that that place was his,
and he did not want him to live over there anymore' (p 106). Formally speaking, as noted, 'Indian settlements' are not to be pre-empted.
Yet the Indian Agent advises the commissioner that the land has been
successfully pre-empted by the man named Hopkins. The chief asks,
reasonably, whether 'it is right for a whiteman to come along and live
in the place where the Indians have been living long years ago. Is it
right – I would like to know – I don't want whitemen to come along
and take the places where the Indian houses are' (108). The commissioner responds that settlers should not preempt land on which Indians
have had their houses for many years, despite the abundant evidence
of this, blandly assuring the chief that they will enquire into this. The
chief, unconvinced, is clear: he wants to 'keep places where we Indians

live nowadays' and thus asks how he can prevent 'a man from coming into the Indian places where they live before?' (108.) The commission chairman's response is instructive:

> The Indian has no right to go on any other man's land to build their houses. The Reserves have been given to them for that purpose, and until additional Reserves are added, he ought not to go on other land and build houses there until such additional reserves have been laid out for you. If you require more land and we agree with that, we can recommend that land be set aside for you by the Government, and they have agreed to do it provided they have the land to do it with.
>
> (108)

Rather than advising the chief as to how he can keep settlers from encroaching on Indigenous land, he assumes that to do so is to threaten settler territoriality. Stay within the geographies assigned to you is the clear message. Rather than acknowledging the patent illegality (in settler terms) of Hopkins' theft, he redirects the onus of obligation to the chief.

The territory of property organizes social relations, empowering some while placing others in spaces of vulnerability. Territoriality can install possession while simultaneously dispossessing others. Such legal choices produce and sustain social hierarchies. Yet Indigenous recognition and opposition to these violent dispossessions are clear in the testimony. Indigenous witnesses recognize that the territoriality of property is differently racialized. One Kwakwak'wakw leader, responding presumably to the commissioner's nostrums regarding the role of the Crown in defending their rights, stated that they were glad to learn that

> there is a Government somewhere that 'holds us and cares for us'. . . . [However] I have not felt like that up to the present time, and when we have had any grievances, we have been told that there was no one to 'back us up' or defend us.
>
> (91)

The racialized differences that allow settlers access to resources while denying them to their traditional owners are visible in the landscape. Chief Johnnie Clark of the Turner Island band (now the Tlowitsis First Nation) noted that his assumption that the island was his was clearly belied by the presence of settlers who had come to the island and 'taken all the timber' (161). 'I have seen white men come and cut the timber off there', he observed, 'just like you would clip the hair off your head'. However, if band members cut a tree, it is taken from them. With this recognition, he is forced to confront 'the immobility to which the native is condemned' (Fanon, 1963, p. 51). As he puts it, this 'has made me know *I am not free to work like other people, and we have just got to keep still*' (161, my emphasis).

Colonial dispossession entails the violent remaking of property relations. Yet, at the same time, Chief Johnnie Clark's testimony alerts us to its irreducible territoriality (Wolfe, 2006, p. 389). Settler assertions of sovereign prerogative rest on the 'exclusive right to . . . decide who can come and who – must or may not – stay within their claimed territorial boundaries' (Saito, 2015, p. 47). As such, Johnnie Clark has 'got to keep still'. As Fanon notes, 'the first thing which the native learns is to stay in his place, and not to go beyond certain limits' (Fanon, 1963, p. 52). Such powerful geographies continue to sustain ongoing dispossessive territorializations on Indigenous lands.

5

Fortifying territory

'[H]ere your house stands alone in the middle of all your little world', promised Dymock, the seventeenth-century English pro-enclosure advocate noted in chapter 3, defended by a bridge or gate so 'strong and stanch that I might let in what I would; but that nothing might get in without my leave' (Hartlib, 1653, p. 20). In his opening statements in the 2018 trial of Gerald Stanley, the Saskatchewan farmer who was found not guilty in the murder of young Cree man Colten Boushie, defence lawyer Scott Spencer told the jury that, '[f]or farm people, your yard is your castle. That's part of the story here' (Starblanket & Hunt, 2018). At work in both examples is a particularly powerful territorial trope, that of private property as a domestic castle.

Territory is not simply an outcome of property's relationality but a particularly strategic resource for its realization. Property works through territory, not on it. As noted previously, this includes the manner in which territory becomes 'a way of seeing' (Brighenti, 2006, p. 69; Thompson, 2007). We are encouraged to 'see' property, it seems, as if it were a fortified home (Atkinson & Blandy, 2017). Gurney (1999, p. 1713) notes the routine invocation of the metaphor (here reframed as 'an Englishman's home is his castle') as a stock phrase, serving as part of a homeowners' 'web of culture':

> [T]he imagery conveyed of impregnable ramparts, familial heraldry and a secured drawbridge vividly underpins the ideologies of independence, identity and security so frequently associated with home-ownership. . . . As a mode of thinking about home-ownership, it attaches great importance to the actual and assumed rights of people to defend their property, whether this be in relation to visual, spatial or aural breaches of a metaphorical moat.

DOI: 10.4324/9781003253389-5

Figure 5.1 'Inside of our brains'.
Source: From sobelow.org; reproduced with permission.

The idea of the private home as like a castle can be linked to *Semayne's Case* in 1604, reported by Edward Coke, in which the Sheriff of London entered a house to seize possessions to cover a personal debt. Although the court ruled that state officials may enter into the space of the home when for lawful purposes, the expectation was that they would announce their purpose (this became the so-called 'knock and announce' rule). That aside, it is Coke's opening that is remembered: 'That the house of every one is to him as his castle and fortress, as well as for his defence against injury and violence, as for his repose . . . is a thing precious and favoured in law'.[1]

1 *Semayne's Case* 1604 5 Co Rep 91a at 91b, 77 ER 194 at 195

The castle metaphor has been described as the 'oldest and most deeply rooted principles in Anglo-American jurisprudence' (Hafetz, 2002, p. 175) and one that continues to resonate. A century after Coke, Blackstone (1769/1979c, p. 223) could intone that 'the law of England has so particular and tender a regard to the immunity of a man's house, that it stiles it his castle, and will never suffer it to be violated with impunity.' A judge in an early eighteenth-century English case also offered the comforting maxim that 'the law bounds everyman's property and is his fence'.[2]

The symbolic territorialization of property through the castle metaphor has travelled into other areas of law, such as privacy. Although it could be conceived of in many ways, privacy is frequently defined in relation to territorial control, and the presumed benefits of private property in securing the 'right to be let alone' (Warren & Brandeis, 1890):

> The right to be alone includes choice about, and control over, when one is alone, and, as rights imply corresponding duties, privacy must be seen as a socially created and respected right to control when and where one appears to others. It is, however, importantly distinct from mere isolation or solitude, for privacy here involves more than simply being on your own; *it entails power over the space which surrounds one.*
>
> (Squires, 1994, p. 390, my emphasis).

Intellectual property is also often likened to property in land, in turn, imagined as a territory governed by notions of trespass.[3]

This and related symbolic territorializations, such as the white picket fence, shape the way in which we think about the work property does in the world. Territorial imaginaries can become powerfully ideological in this sense. Robertson (1995) notes that the territorialized image of the private home:

> is one of the powerful paradigms at work organizing our thinking about private property rights and duties. By this I mean that when

---

2 *Star v Rookesby*, 1 Salk 336, 91 Eng Rep 295, 3 Bl Comm. 309, 1711

3 *Compagnie Générale des Établissements Michelin-Michelin & Cie v. National Automobile, Aerospace, Transportation and General Workers Union of Canada (CAW-Canada)*, [1997] 2 FC 306. Thanks to Teresa Scassa for this information

people consider what the rights of a property owner should be, and whether any suggested changes to property rights should be approved of, they apply the proposed rights and changes to the example of the family home to see if they fit, or feel right. We think that we should largely be free to deal with our homes as we see fit, and that we should be free from government intrusions into our homes.

(282)

As such, all property owners, be they ever so base, are like a baron in his castle. The barons, however, have proved adept at mobilizing castles for their own purposes, often to defend themselves against the interests of the lowborn. As Robertson (1995, p. 282) notes;

Large business corporations hitch a ride on these deeply felt sentiments and effectively mimic the family home when they demand to be treated the same way. They justify their ability to close down plants, without having to involve in the decision the employees or communities affected, on the basis that the plant is their private property to deal with as they see fit. They resist various government attempts to verify compliance with anti-pollution legislation and workers' safety legislation on the grounds that this constitutes an unreasonable search under the American Bill of Rights.

The relational powers of private property owners (or what I refer to as 'acting' in the property space) also rely on the defensive territoriality of the castle. Evictions, for example, rest on the powerful concept of exclusive possession, defined as a 'conclusion of law defining the nature and status of a particular relationship of control by a person over land' (Gray & Gray, 2009, p. 105). As noted in Chapter 2, possession is thus understood as a straightforward expression of territorial control. Similarly, as noted in the discussion of early modern English enclosure, the ancient action of trespass, once a general tort relating to harm, has become sharply territorialized, echoing the powers of the lord in the castle to expel unwanted invaders. Trespass sustains 'the concept of personal and territorial inviolability which remains deeply embedded in the history of the common law' (Gray & Gray, 2009, p. 4). 'Our law holds the property of every man so sacred', intoned Lord Camden in 1765, 'that no man can set his foot upon his neighbour's close without his leave'.[4] The territorial inviolability of owned land from the spatial incursion of uninvited strangers is held to be 'a fundamental principle going to the root of our social order'.[5] While there may be cases in which trespass to land can be justified (for example, the preservation of life), these are unusual. 'It remains the legal prerogative of property owners to exclude all others from their land, regardless of the reason for exercising this veto right – whether the decision is based on spite, opportunism, or mere caprice' (Depoorter, 2011, p. 1098). So, for example, the travails of homelessness do not constitute a social necessity that would override it: the castle's inviolability must be sustained. As Gray and Gray (2009, pp. 1270–1271) note, common law courts have refused to accept a wide range of public interest concerns as justifying unconsented intrusion:

> Unavailing excuses have included bona fide protest against the commissioning of a nuclear waste dump, concern about the development of the nuclear industry, sincere indignation about proven nuclear contamination, a desire to stop a defence contractor's 'war crimes', opposition to logging in ecologically sensitive forest areas, support for environmental and planning legislation, abhorrence of battery hen farming, peaceful opposition to road-building proposals, and a desire to preserve dignified buildings from demolition.

Trespass does not require proof that the trespasser used force to cross the line or did so with a possessory intent (Depoorter, 2011, p. 1096). As Blackstone noted:

> every man's land is in the eye of the law enclosed and set apart from his neighbour's; and that either by a visible and material fence, as one field is divided from another by a hedge; or by an in ideal invisible boundary, existing only in the contemplation of the law, as when one man's Land adjoins to another's in the same field.
>   (1768/1979b, p. 209)

The distinctively territorial dimension of trespass is evident in its distinction from nuisance. While trespass concerns the protection of a

---

4 *Entick v Carrington* (1765) 95 ER 807 at 817
5 *Reference re and Application for an Authorisation* (1984) 5 DLR (4th) 601 at 616.

property interest from the physical crossing of a line, it is not concerned with other property interests, such as the enjoyment of a property free from other annoyances, which is captured by nuisance law (Rowbotham, 1978, p. 119). Trespass to land is actionable regardless of the extent of the spatial incursion, without any necessary showing of injury or damage to the claimant. Trespass to land is quintessentially territorial: merely to cross the boundary (even, sometimes, unintentionally) is to commit a trespass: 'Accordingly, the midnight streaker who dashes unseen across the lawn of another, and who merely bends a few blades of grass in the process, is guilty of the tort of trespass' (Merrill & Smith, 2007, p. 1871). Vast swathes of territory, even at considerable distances from obvious markers of occupation and private habitation, are thus encased in the resultant legal force-field, over which law-abiding subjects dare not cross.

As well as shaping the work of law, it is also important to reflect on the ways in which the castle metaphor might shape broader conceptions of social relationality. This reflects the specific work of territorialization as a classificatory and ordering device. Spatial classifications function at an unspoken level, beyond consciousness and language (Cresswell, 1996, pp. 152–153), projecting a seemingly objective inside/outside, either/or imaginary on the world (Delaney, 2010, pp. 138–139). This can be consequential, militating against a richer and ethically informed understanding of the relationality of property and territory. The castle metaphor relies upon a spatial logic of defensive boundaries, with a sharp divide between a secure inside and a threatening outside. Through its military and feudal invocations, it invokes notions of lordship, dominion, and sovereignty. McClain (1995) notes the use of related metaphors in U.S. jurisprudence, including 'shelter', 'enclave', 'insulated enclosure', 'inviolate place', and 'oasis'. Sheltered imaginatively behind the towering ramparts, we can easily overlook the fact that the walls themselves are effectively built by the collective (Suk, 2008).

The effect is to convey 'an image of property as a source of security whose sacredness acts as a barrier even to the state' (Nedelsky, 1990, p. 162). Dominant conceptions of property rely on the installation and defence of hard boundaries around the propertied self. Autonomy is imagined as predicated on the maintenance of a bounded zone from which others – the state, nonowners, and other owners – are to be expelled. Property law famously 'draws a circle' around the private individual 'within which he is master' (Reich, 1964, p. 771). This invites a meagre view of property, selfhood, and the collective, whereby autonomy requires the independence and separation that private property promises that:

> individual autonomy is to be achieved by erecting a wall (of rights) between the individual and those around him. Property ... is ... the central symbol for this vision of autonomy, for it can both literally and figuratively provide the necessary walls.
>
> (Nedelsky, 1989, p. 12)

This can be a problem when '[o]ur focus on boundary turns our attention away from relationship and thus away from the true sources and consequences of the patterns of power that property constitutes' (Nedelsky, 1990, p. 177). This misrepresents the actual workings of property. Singer (2006) argues that the castle metaphor has the effect of confining property's relational reach to a limited space. The central question it invites, he suggests, is what it means to stay within one's borders. The presumption is that the owner has a right to engage in self-regarding acts within his or her own borders but not outside. However, actions inside the borders, even if self-regarding, can have negative effects on others outside the border. Put another way, the castle metaphor suppresses 'the ways in which one castle can be used to invade another' (318). The fixation on the castle metaphor obscures the inherent relationality to property, in other words.

As the self is spatialized, so is property itself. Rather than a bundle of relations, 'property' becomes territorialized, imagined as the object of property itself, rather than the relations that make it possible. Thus it is that we commonly talk about 'buying property' or 'my property' as if it were a bounded parcel of land.

The social power of the castle metaphor, perhaps, can be traced to the work of reification, or of the manner in which social relations are easily misrepresented as objective things. A castle is undeniably an objective thing. Property, however, is not. Yet when we imaginatively territorialize property as a castle, we turn the play of social relations and power into an inert, external object. Precisely because space appears to us moderns as something 'out there', beyond us, rather than a social product, so territories tend to:

> convey the appearance of durability to the fragmented segments of our life-worlds. They appear to arrest, freeze, fix, concretize the

play of power. This appearance underpins the experience of social space as static condition, as cause, reason, or justification for how to comport ourselves.

(Delaney, 2010, p. 139)

This becomes consequential in the ethical evaluation of the power sustained by property relations.

Robert Sack suggests that when power relations become territorialized, we depersonalize power relations, arguing that 'territory can be used to displace attention between the controller and the controlled as when we say... "you can't do that here"' (1986, p. 33). The result, Sack argues, is that interactions between people can be seen as caused by territory itself, as a separate object, rather than the interpersonal relations at the centre of power. Rather than confronting the interpersonal conflicts between my neighbour, I build a 'spite fence' at our mutual boundary. Rather than recognizing the social violences that sustain my fee simple property right, I blame the spatial transgression of the Travellers camped out on my grouse estate when I call the police. As a result, 'territory appears as the agent doing the controlling' (Sack, 1986, p. 33).

What is needed metaphorically, Singer argues, is to step beyond the castle through the recognition that property entails obligations rather than absolute rights:

> property is not just an individual entitlement but a social institution involving many owners. . . . Property rights cannot be fixed entitlements but are contingent, to some extent, on the social context in which they are exercised.
>
> (2000, p. 31)

It becomes interesting, therefore, to imagine alternative metaphors to the castle. Peñalver, (2005) opposes the castle-like trope of 'exit' in relation to property and advocates for a view of property as 'entrance' or as one that 'does not view property principally as a boundary separating individuals from one another but primarily as a means of joining individuals to each other in community' (1894).

Yet the castle still stands. Indeed, it has been strengthened in the service of a broader logic of fortification, neoliberal individualization, and the racialized cultivation of anxiety and fear. We see this, for example, in relation to lawful defence against trespass. For a castle is not just a passive space of separation and security. Etymologically, the word 'castle' derives from the word 'to cut'.[6] Castles, like knives, are to be used as weapons. While the common law has long required landowners to retreat from a territorial incursion rather than respond with lethal violence, Coke's castle doctrine provides legal protection for those who use force to defend their home, providing there is no intent to kill or grievously harm the trespasser (Yeo, 2011). Blackstone argued that to intrude into the home was to violate a man's natural 'right of habitation' (1769/1979c, p. 223), grounded in the defence of home and property.

Blackstone made clear the distinction between the home and a public place, however. If in the latter, where there was a duty to retreat, the home was different:

> A crossing of the home boundary triggered permission for the attacked individual to use force in the way a state normally does to defend its borders. Intrusion into the home thus placed the intruder beyond the protection of the law and suspended the state monopoly on violence.
>
> (Suk, 2009, p. 59)

Since 2005, driven by lobbying from the National Rifle Association (NRA), many American states have embraced more aggressive versions of the castle doctrine, responding to white paranoia driven by racialized anxieties of 'stranger danger' combined with post 9–11 fears of the 'enemy within' (Light, 2015). Florida was the first to modify the existing castle doctrine, expanding the circumstances in which the use of deadly force in the home is permitted (notably, allowing the occupant to kill the intruder even when there is no reasonable fear of the safety of the occupant), and granting immunity to those who exercise it. As Suk (2009) shows, the preamble to the law draws a sharp line between 'law-abiding people' inside their homes and 'intruders and attackers' who threaten the castle. For the NRA, '[t]his law is about affirming that your home is your castle, and, in Florida, you have a right to be absolutely safe inside its walls' (quoted in Suk, 2009, p. 76).

Metaphorically, however, the space of the castle became more generalized as American courts abandoned the duty to retreat in public places. Thus a person could lawfully 'stand his ground' to kill in self-defence in any space to which they had a lawful right, in a radical

---

6 www.etymonline.com/word/castle

extension of the castle doctrine. As Suk (2009) notes, this was sustained by ideologies of the 'true man' who did not flee from a threat but defended his honour and protected his wife and family. Such gendered norms were closely tied to racialized anxieties concerning perceived assaults on white property: 'Hegemonic masculine ideals of self-defense were therefore inextricable from the white supremacist logic of violent exclusionary citizenship that concentrated political and economic power securely into the hands of white men' (Light, 2015, p. 295)

It also relied on a territorialized rights-framing, Suk (2009, p. 63) notes, in which a boundary-crossing constituted a violation of a man's rights, presumably echoing the notion of boundary-crossing as an affront or harm to the individual, as discussed previously. The true man should and could stand his ground in a space to which he had a lawful right. The home as castle, of course, was the paradigmatic example. But if one had a lawful right to be in other places, it seemed to follow that one also had a right to stand one's ground there also:

> The home, traditionally the only place where there was no duty to retreat, became the means to perform the expansion to the rule of no duty to retreat. The true man's role, to protect the home and family, was a model for the broader self-defense right of the true man.
>
> (Suk, 2009, p. 63)

Stand-your-ground (SYG) laws thus extend the territorial logic of the castle doctrine beyond the home, muddying 'the underlying purpose of self-defence so that it was no longer clear whether self-defence was primarily about protection of human life or protection of property, liberty, and honour' (Weisbord, 2018, p. 358). As of 2021, twenty-eight U.S. states have adopted SYG laws, and an additional eight states have statutes that expand the right to stand your ground in certain places beyond the home (Coalition to Stop Gun Violence, 2021). Following the Black Lives Matter protests, several states have expanded SYG laws to allow individuals to shoot at looters destroying property (Coalition to Stop Gun Violence, 2021).

SYG laws, like the castle doctrine, are notionally neutral as to their beneficiaries. Indeed, the implication is that all property owners and legal occupants, regardless of race or income, are entitled to its protections. However, as noted, the impulse to weaponize the castle cannot be detached from racist anxieties regarding those imagined as threats to the citadel. It is in this light that we can understand its appeal in former slave states. Dirlam et al. (2021) found a state's vigilante and racist past proved explanatory in the uptake of SYG laws, likening them to a 'New Jim Crow'. Commentators also note the importance of local histories of racism and forms of vigilantist 'self-help' targeting Black people in explaining the uptake of SYG laws (Light, 2015; Singer, 2021)

The differentiated outcome is brutally predictable, as the murders of Trayvon Martin and Ahmaud Arbury reveal. Since the codification of SYG laws, the average number of legally 'justifiable' homicides increased by 725% in Kentucky, 200% in Florida, and 83% in Georgia (Bell, 2019, p. 915). More whites own guns than do Blacks, particularly in the South, where SYG laws predominate. Blacks face more severe penalties for using self-defence, especially when against white aggressors (Bell, 2019, p. 924). One 2013 study found that white shooters who killed African-Americans were legally justified 38% of the time, while African-American shooters who killed white victims were only justified 3.3% of the time (Bell, 2019, p. 924), reflecting deep-seated presumptions of the dangerous black man: 'The bottom line is that under Stand Your Ground black life has less value than white life' (Russell-Brown, 2015, p. 137) Light (2015) argues that the technically race-neutral conceptions of 'reasonable threat' justifying lethal force in SYG laws 'empower the DIY armed citizen with broad justification for immediate lethal responses to perceived intrusions into spaces considered white' (296). As a result:

> the white castle might potentially be anywhere, including a public street... [Stand-your-ground] laws are the nation's new system of legalized homicide by which the sanctity of white property can remain self-possessed.
>
> (296).

SYG laws have received considerable attention. However, even absent explicit fortification, the castle of property can still become a site of violence. As noted in the introduction to this chapter, it was invoked in relation to the 2016 death of young Red Pheasant Cree man Colten Boushie in rural Saskatchewan, Canada. Colten Boushie was fatally shot in the back of the head by Gerald Stanley after he and his friends entered Stanley's farm. Stanley was found not guilty of second-degree murder by an all-white jury, relying on the defence that the killing was an accident. Although his defence did not directly invoke the castle doctrine, territorial tropes of trespass, coloured with racist anxieties concerning Indigenous people, mixed with claims of the reasonableness of the use of a gun: 'property and trespass were invoked to intersect with, and compound, racism and colonialism' (Flynn & Wagner, 2020, p. 361). The white farm was imagined as a castle, threatened by Indigenous trespassers. Stanley's fear of Indigenous youths and their status as trespassers was thus deemed presumptively reasonable.

Deeply racialized and gendered, the settler 'castle' evident in the case relies on a powerful set of narratives, opposing the domestic security of the home from the immanent threat of intrusion always just outside the walls, justifying the use of violence. But what, ask Indigenous scholars Starblanket and Hunt (2018), if we invert the narrative and frame settler property as an intrusion?:

> How can we reconcile the inhospitable notion of 'intrusion' that then rationalizes settler violence with the nearly inconceivable acts of generosity that Indigenous peoples have extended and continue to extend in agreeing to share the land through treaty?
>
> (no page)

The castle trope, therefore, serves as a powerful ideological prop, sustaining settler entitlement to mobilize violence to protect settler property.

The production and protection of the legal castle are clearly racialized. This contradicts the manner in which such protections are presented, for the benefits of the castle are supposedly available to all, as William Pitt argued in Parliament in 1763 (approvingly cited in *Miller v United States*[7]):

> The poorest man may in his cottage bid defiance to all the force of the Crown. It may be frail – its roof may shake – the wind may blow through it – the storm may enter, the rain may enter – but the King of England cannot enter – all his force dares not cross the threshold of the ruined tenement.

Yet there are many who find that their homes do not qualify as castles, legally speaking. Put another way, property over-protects the home of those held up by a property regime while under-valuing those made vulnerable by such a system. Those who do not have secure title to their homes thus often find that their personal rights can be violated by encroachers. Take, for example, constitutional privacy protections under section 8 of the Canadian *Charter of Rights and Freedoms*, whereby '[e]veryone has the right to be secure against unreasonable search or

---

7 *Miller v United States* 357 US 301 (158)

seizure'. As noted previously, liberal privacy is conceptually grounded in the control one has over territory. Squires (1994, p. 392) writes that privacy 'is therefore most often conceptualized as a right with a spatial location'. As privacy is territorialized, so it reaches its apogee in the legal construction of the category of 'home'. Canadian jurisprudence has consistently maintained that when we are in the home, we will enjoy robust expectations of privacy (cf. Hafetz, 2002; McClain, 1995).

But not everyone's home is recognized as a legal 'home'. Couch-surfers, trailer dwellers, and rental locker users, for example, do not enjoy the same protections as those with a more secure title. The legal protections of home are not available to those who live precariously. Take the case of Louis Picard.[8] Mr. Picard's home was on the same stretch of sidewalk in Vancouver's Downtown East Side, where he had lived for two years with his girlfriend in a tent, never leaving the space unattended. In 2018, police seized drugs from his tent without a warrant. At the heart of the resultant case was whether his tent could be characterized as a 'home' for judicial purposes. If so, the tent would afford Mr. Picard a high expectation of privacy under section 8 of the *Charter of Rights and Freedoms*, as absent exceptional circumstances, a search could only be conducted with a warrant.

Not surprisingly, section 8 jurisprudence does not include many cases relating to privacy rights in respect of tents. Justice Lee thus looked to other legal references, including the definition of a 'dwelling house' in section 2 of the *Criminal Code*, which states:

> Dwelling-house means the whole or any part of a building or structure that is kept or occupied as a permanent or temporary residence, and includes (a) a building within the curtilage of a dwelling-house that is connected to it be a doorway or by a covered and enclosed passage-way, and (b) a unit that is designed to be mobile and to be used as a permanent or temporary residence and that is being used as such a residence.[9]

Mr. Picard's description of his experience and his sentiments suggested that his tent was a home under section 2(b) because his tent was his

---

8 *R v Picard*, 2018 BCPC 344. This argument is extended in Ferencz et al. (forthcoming)
9 Ibid. at § 26.

permanent or temporary residence and was designed to be mobile. However, Justice Lee held that it is 'too simplistic to say that any residence or place which a person calls home is automatically a "home" in the legal sense, so as to entitle Mr. Picard to protection from a warrantless search save for exceptional circumstances'.[10] Instead, Justice Lee argued that he needed to consider 'all the circumstances of the particular case when assessing the claim for privacy'.[11]

The circumstance that Justice Lee focused on was whether 'there was a legal right for the occupant to reside on the property upon which lies the residence'.[12] Justice Lee concluded that

> Mr. Picard did not have the legal right to erect a tent on the City sidewalk. He may have put up a tent, and the City may have acquiesced in the presence of the tent, but that did not give Mr. Picard a legal right to place the tent onto City property.[13]

The absence of a real property interest was key in Justice Lee's decision. Mr. Picard was prohibited from putting his tent on city property; therefore, it was not a 'home' for section 8 purposes, and thus his tent could be searched even without a warrant.

According to this distinction, a tent is not a 'home' for legal purposes if the occupant of the tent does not have a secure property interest to the land on which the tent sits. This means that houseless people, by definition, will almost inevitably not have a 'home' in law. The fact that Mr. Picard was homeless, living on city land, means, therefore, that he was legally 'homeless'.

The solution, it seems, is simple. Mr. Picard needs property in the land he occupies. Similarly, if SYG laws favour white property owners, private property rights should be extended to everyone. We should all have castles we can call our own. If Mr. Picard has a legal right to occupy space, he has a 'home'. Only then may he 'bid defiance to all the force of the crown', as William Pitt put it. With title, he will no longer be governed by the private property right of others and will have somewhere he can call his own, from which others can

---

10 Ibid. at § 38.
11 Ibid. at § 36.
12 Ibid. at § 39.
13 Ibid. at § 40.

be excluded. This, broadly, is Essert's (2017) argument: 'The homeless are homeless because they lack any right to decide how things will be as between them and others in the space where they live. In other words, they are homeless because they lack property' (274–275). The obvious Leftist temptation to dismiss private property is misguided, he argues, for, without private property rights, all of us would be, effectively, houseless, in that we would lack rights with respect to land and objects that were not in physical possession. The solution, then, is to ensure that everyone, including the houseless, has such property rights.

Such an argument has an ethical appeal. Arguing that the solution to houselessness is simply shelter, for example, ignores the ways in which such options – such as homeless shelters or 'supportive housing' – frequently negate residents' ability to control access to such spaces in ways that deny their agency and minimize their freedom. The argument also has a logical appeal: if the condition of houselessness is a lack of control over one's space and property rights grant control, it would seem to follow that property rights should be extended to those who lack them. Protecting the rights of houseless people to their personal possessions – often seized illegally or illegitimately by those with entrenched property interests – also seems eminently reasonable (Blomley et al., 2020c).

But there are reasons to be cautious of this argument. In particular, of course, it reproduces the dominant view of (private) property as a territorial redoubt. This effaces the work of property in producing the very precarity that it is now supposed to secure. Houselessness is not an outlier but a product of the property space (Blomley, 2009). It also ignores the role of these powerfully entrenched and deeply territorial metaphors and tropes in upholding dominant propertied interests, serving to advance whiteness. It overlooks the close entanglement of the dominant territorial logic with neoliberalism, the corporate manufacture of fear, and the increasing assertion of social individualism (Atkinson & Blandy, 2017). It also falsely assumes that only private property can secure autonomy and security. The powerful work of collective property, albeit informal, in securing houseless people's interests in a tent encampment needs to be acknowledged. For both property and territory can be differently configured. It is to this theme that I now turn.

6

Opening up territory

Sam Wallman's 'comic about land' paints a powerful picture of the work of property's exclusive territoriality and its role in conflict, colonial violence, extraction, and sovereign powers. Yet despite its oppressions, Wallman notes, 'minor interventions occur on every corner/ Animals transgress the very borders we hold so dear/Indigenous people resist the pull of extractive relationships/Queers have sex inside of the cracks, staking out a space for intimacy'.

In this final chapter, my goal is to demonstrate the 'cracks' within the dominant territorial logic. I seek to show, firstly, that even orthodox legal practice does not conform to the narrowly defined spatial parameters of the ownership model. This is, in large part, I argue secondly, because of the continued contestation of property's territoriality. In particular, those rendered precarious by the 'property space', such as squatters, civil rights activists, sit-down strikers, Indigenous activists, and houseless people, continuously contest property's territory. Their precarious status, in many senses, is shaped by the exclusion generated by the territorialization of dominant property relations. Their struggles, moreover, centre not only on property relations but crucially also on their territorialization.

Cracks, Jacque, and Shack

Lois and Harvey Jacque, a retired farming couple, owned 170 acres near Wilke Lake in Wisconsin. In 1993, their neighbour bought a mobile home from Steenberg Homes Inc. Direct delivery of the mobile home to the neighbour was difficult, as it entailed the use of a snow-covered private road with a sharp curve. On several occasions, Steenberg asked the Jacques if they would allow access to their property to expedite delivery to the neighbour, offering financial compensation. The Jacques (who were sensitive about having others access

DOI: 10.4324/9781003253389-6

Figure 6.1 'Minor interventions'.

Source: From sobelow.org; reproduced with permission.

their land due to an earlier adverse possession case) refused. Steenberg summarily ignored their veto. In court, one of the employees testified that the assistant manager for Steenberg told him: 'I don't give a _____ what [Mr. Jacque] said, just get the home in there any way you can'. Steenberg's employees thus used a Bobcat to plough a path on Jacques' snow-covered field and hauled the home across to the neighbour's lot. Mr. Jacque called the Sheriff, who issued a $30 citation to the assistant manager. The Jacques commenced a tort action, seeking compensatory and punitive damages from Steenberg. The jury awarded the Jacques $100,000 in punitive damages, but the lower court found this was excessive and awarded only nominal damages. The Jacques appealed this decision.[1]

Mr. Tedesco employed migrant workers in New Jersey. Frank Tejeras was a field worker for a nonprofit organization seeking to provide health services for migrant workers. He sought to enter Tedesco's farm to pick up an injured worker and take them to the hospital to remove stitches. Peter Shack was an attorney with another nonprofit organization that provided legal advice and representation for workers. Shack wished to investigate a report that a worker employed by Tedesco had been injured and was unable to receive wages.

This followed general complaints of the intimidation of antipoverty officials by farmers in the area. No trespassing signs had sprouted in the region, with officials and organizers 'run out of camps by gun-wielding farmers' (Sullivan, 1970, p. 19) seeking to keep officials from assisting migrant farm workers, many of them Black and Puerto Rican. Officials warned that farmers were using territorial trespass powers against workers by isolating one camp from another so that any wage or living improvements were kept secret, thus using 'the camp isolation as a "chilling" weapon to maintain tight control' (Sullivan, 1970, p. 19).

Nevertheless, Shack and Tejeras entered Tedesco's farm without his permission. He confronted them and asked their purpose. Tedesco then offered to find the men but insisted that any consultation relating to legal matters would have to take place in his presence. Tejeras and Shack refused, saying that they should see the men alone. According to a *New York Times* reporter who had accompanied Shack and Tejeras, Tedesco had said that even President Nixon would not be allowed to see the conditions of migrant workers on his farm. He threatened the

1 *Jacque v Steenberg Homes, Inc.* N.W. 2d 154 (Wis. 1997)

reporter, 'I'll smash you for this, I'm going to get you for this. This is my property. You can't come in here looking around' (Sullivan, 1970, p. 19). Tedesco called a state trooper who charged Shack and Tejeras with violation of a trespass statute. They appealed their convictions in the Municipal and County Court and challenged the constitutionality of the trespass statute.[2]

Two familiar territorial tales, then. In both cases, people had crossed a line and were resisted by a property owner. Strikingly, however, the two stories ended very differently. In the *Jacques* case, when the landowners appealed the lower court's refusal to award punitive damages, the Supreme Court of Wisconsin agreed with the property owners wholeheartedly. The right to exclude is one of the most important and venerable sticks in the private property bundle, and such a right is hollow without state support, the court insisted, quoting Cohen (1954) at § 22:

> [T]hat is property to which the following label can be attached:
> To the world:
> Keep off X unless you have my permission, which I may grant or withhold.
> Signed: Private Citizen
> Endorsed: The state.

The trespass (although causing no apparent physical damage to the Jacques' land) nevertheless constituted harm, the court argued, for it signalled an indifference to the rights of the owner. Society has an interest in punishing and deterring intentional trespassers. Landowners should feel secure in knowing that trespassers will be punished. In an interesting echo of the Stand Your Ground laws noted previously, the court also argued that without secure confidence in the state's role in securing the castle, landowners may pursue 'self-help' options. Moreover, if punitive damages are not applied, what is to stop Steenberg Homes or those who 'contemplate trespassing on the land of another' (§ 28) from continuing to ignore property boundaries in pursuit of their own interest? To ignore this 'implicitly tells them that they are free to go where they please, regardless of the landowner's wishes' (§ 28).

The Jacques' castle was thus secured by the court, reinstating the punitive damages levied against Steenberg Homes. Trespass harms

---

2 *State v. Shack*, 277 A.2d 369, 372 (N.J. 1971)

society and the owner, and should be appropriately punished, even absent any physical harm. What, then, of the intentional trespass on to the private domain of another farmer, Mr. Tedesco? The Supreme Court of New Jersey was comfortable with certain orthodox aspects of property's territoriality. The owner should be free to pursue his farming activities without interference. Solicitors and peddlers do not have the right to enter his land without his invitation. However, trespass is not at issue here, the court argues. Unlike the *Jacques* case, the dispute cannot be resolved by playing the trump card of ownership. Rather, the dispute should be framed as a conflict between the interests of Mr. Tedesco and multiple others affected by his actions. Property implicates multiple people (the owner, the public, the state, the migrant worker) and should be assessed accordingly, the court argued:

> Property rights serve human values. They are recognized to that end, and are limited by it. Title to real property cannot include dominion over the destiny of persons the owner permits to come upon the premises. Their well-being must remain the paramount concern of a system of law.

Property rights cannot be reduced exclusively to the interests of the owner, in other words. Put another way, multiple people have a legitimate property interest in this dispute, not just the owner.

Similarly, property's territory is understood not as a carapace protecting the solitary owner but as a relational nexus, implicating multiple people. The court worries that the owner's territorial powers can serve to spatially separate migrant workers, an already disadvantaged 'community within but apart from the local scene. They are rootless and isolated'. Government has expressed an interest in coming to their aid through the introduction of multiple programs and initiatives. However, '[t]hese ends would not be gained if the intended beneficiaries could be insulated from efforts to reach them'. They can only be reached by physical contact from people such as Shack and Tejeras. An owner may have some oversight regarding such contacts, but they have no absolute power to ban access. To do so would violate the

> opportunity to live with dignity and to enjoy associations customary among our citizens. These rights are too fundamental to be denied on the basis of an interest in real property and too fragile to be left to the unequal bargaining strength of the parties.

Shack is, in many senses, an unusual case. However, it is too easy to dismiss it as the exception that proves the rule. For if we look more carefully at property law, we find not only exceptions to the dominant territorial model but clear indications that this model is one of only many forms. As noted previously, the purposes that property serve are many and diverse, despite the wishes of many scholars, who insist that they have discovered the singular function that property sustains (utility, 'improvement', etc.). For property, as practised by lawyers and lived in everyday life, should not be understood as 'a monistic institution revolving around the idea of exclusion' (Dagan, 2021, p. 81). While some aspects of property practice can certainly be understood according to this logic, large parts of property practice are designed to facilitate relationships of cooperation, communal life, and collective flourishing (Alexander, 1997; Singer, 2000). Property is thus not just about:

> vindicating the rights of autonomous excluders cloaked in Black-stonian armours of sole and despotic dominion, but rather about creating governance institutions that manage potential conflicts of interest among individuals who are all stakeholders in one resource or a given set of resources. These dramas of property law occur, literally, within property; they deal with the internal life of property rather than with its foreign affairs.
>
> (Dagan, 2021, p. 82)

As an interaction device, then, the property of territory is not simply a space from which others are to be excluded, legally speaking, but rather one that can be designed to facilitate forms of inclusion or access. Metaphorically, property's territory is often like a gate, in other words, not just a wall (Peñalver, 2005). Examples include nuisance law (empowering the state to access private property in the interests of public aesthetics and hygiene); the law of adverse possession (placing a time limit on an owner's right to exclude); the doctrine of public or private necessity (requiring an owner to allow others onto their property in moments of extreme need); the law of aeroplane over-flights (converting aerospace above a certain height into a state property); the public trust doctrine (that may require that certain privately owned places be made accessible to the public) and the right to roam (allowing recreational access to certain wilderness areas). Kelly (2014) also points out that owners have the right to include as well as exclude. A landlord has the right to make land available to renters, who have the right to invite guests without the landlord's permission, for example. Kelly offers a useful thought experiment to alert us to the pervasive and important dimensions of property inclusion: Imagine a world in which you cannot include others in the use, possession, or enjoyment of your property, and others cannot include you in their property. Such a world 'differs dramatically from the inter-related and inclusive world in which we live, work, and play. Inclusion is critical because human beings depend on each other, not only to survive, but to flourish' (2014, pp. 870–871).

For scholars such as Singer (2000), these should not be treated as exceptions to the norm but as pervasive manifestations of the complicated relationality at work across property boundaries, predicated on property's service in advancing not only individual entitlement but also inter-relational obligation. U.S. public accommodations law is one such example, he notes. It is a well-established principle in American law that owners who serve the public, through establishments such as malls or restaurants, have an obligation to allow access to their property without inappropriate discrimination. This has been buttressed by federal law, such as the 1964 Civil Rights Act. Singer argues, however, that the principle of public accommodation should not be seen as a balance between property and equality. Rather public accommodations law not only curtails the exclusionary powers of the owner but transfers one of these rights to the non-owner, framing a right of access to land possessed by another as a property right, comparable to an easement. The relation between access and exclusion, therefore, should be seen as internal to the property system itself. The territory of property, therefore, is not simply a space of absolute exclusion. It may also serve as a space of relative inclusion. There are doors built into property's castle.

Property's outlaws

There is thus a rich realm of law that reveals that the 'contours of the right to exclude are both more complex and interesting than the homeowner's . . . claim of an unqualified right to exclude allows' (Alexander & Peñalver, 2012, p. 134). Property is multivalent, serving multiple ends, both individual and collective (Singer, 2000), as noted previously. But we should not simply assume that this diversity is a function of some quasi-mystical internal genius embedded within property law. Property is a product of a social order. Most often, as we have seen here, it is designed to hold up the interests of dominant economic and social interests. But it is also a product of social struggle and contestation. Such struggles turn both on the form and organization of the bundle of rights attached to private property, on the associated territorial relations at play, and the multiple ends that property serves.

Such diversity is a response to a long history of struggles against dominant territorializations of property and their exclusionary logic. The status of those who resist is, in many senses, shaped by the exclusion generated in part by property's territory. Their struggles, moreover, centre not only on property relations but crucially also on their territorial form. Put another way, they can be thought of as outlaws in that property law has placed them in a space of heightened vulnerability, in which they are subject to the predations and exclusions of those whose property interests are more securely protected (Blomley & The Right to Remain Collective, 2021).

They can also be seen as articulating a form of commoning, counterposed to the individualism of private property. To the extent that the freedom of nonowners is compromised by the owner's right to exclude, they can be said to have a common right not to be excluded (Blomley, 2016c, 2020b). This is not a 'right to be included', in which the goal is to become vested in the power of the private owner to exclude others. Nor is it simply a matter of access to collectively held land, important though that may be. Rather, it can be understood as a counter to the right to exclude, its territorial manifestations, and the manner in which this negates human freedom and possibility, particularly for those who the property space render vulnerable: the poor, the working class, and the racialized. These struggles have often proved instrumental in recalibrating the 'property space' and its territoriality. The fierce (and ongoing) struggle against land enclosure was noted previously. In what follows, I offer a few additional examples of property outlaws engaged in struggles against dominant property regimes and their territoriality.

Squatters

Squatters, by definition, have a particular relationship to property and territory. Squatting reflects a fundamental need, reflecting the dominance of a regime of territorialized private property and a landscape of capitalist exclusion. To the extent that a place is governed by private property rules, squatting enacts the common right not to be excluded. In so doing, squatters challenge a systemic denial of space by taking their own. For Vasudevan (2015, p. 349), squatting should be thought of as a form of 'makeshift urbanism' reliant on a 'political imaginary characterized by a provisional and precarious openness to the possibilities of assembling and developing other alternative urbanisms out of the very matter and stuff of inequality, displacement and dispossession'. The San Francisco squatting organization 'Homes Not Jails' answers the question 'Why squat?' with the simple answer: 'To survive', noting that '[i]f food, clothing and shelter are basic necessities for life, to forcibly take those away from people is to prevent their survival. Any act to resist this is, by definition, self-defence' (Homes Not Jails, 2013, pp. 2, 3). Brazilian housing activists make a related claim: 'Enquanto morar for um privilégio, ocupar é um direito' ('as long as private property is a privilege, to occupy is a right'). To exist is to take up space. To the extent that property denies space, it must be contested. As Singer puts it: 'If property law does not ensure access to property somewhere, then the law has outlawed your existence. It has made a person illegal' (Singer, 2015, pp. 945–946). As Neuwirth (2005, p. 311) puts it, squatters

> are excluded so they take, but they are not taking an abstract right, they are taking an actual place; a place to lay their heads . . . this act – to challenge society's denial of place by taking one of your own – is an assertion in being in a world that routinely denies people the dignity and the validity inherent in a home.

Homes Not Jails provides detailed information on how to take 'an actual place'. Not surprisingly, such information is highly territorialized, offering detailed advice on how to identify buildings that are potential targets, how to physically access one, how to deal with neighbours and police, and how to perform territorialized presence and permanence.

Echoing the multivalent nature of property noted previously, the assumed right of the private owner to exclude unwanted occupants in the case of squatting, for example, is far from certain within judicial practice. McCarthy (2014) expresses considerable anxiety regarding 'squatter's rights' (ironic, of course, in the context of settler land policy), noting the manner in which squatters may invoke adverse possession to buttress their claim to private property. The supposedly certain categories of private owner, trespasser, and squatter in the property space are far from stable; she fears: 'The legal differences between squatting and trespassing and the applications of the laws have resulted in unclear understanding among owners of property and even among legal scholars' (168).

Sit down strikers

Labour-based struggles and activism, and associated forms of regulation, also turn on property relations and the territorial dimensions of the workplace. Workers not only sell their labour but also usually do so upon land owned by the employer. Labour activists thus must negotiate or confront the territorialized right to exclude of the employer. The conditional rights won by labour unions are shaped by generations of such struggles.

One telling moment comes from the 'sit-down' strikes of the U.S. in the late 1930s. Driven by claims for workplace democracy and union recognition, workers in auto plants and retail outlets struggled with the challenges of picketing outside the workplace, easily broken up by the authorities, and the employer's use of scab labour inside the workplace. The spatial solution was to 'sit down' in protest at the work site itself. The sit-down was thus 'the transfer of the picket line into the plant' (Pope, 2006, p. 81), according to one supporter. Between 1936 and 1939, American workers staged some 583 sit-down strikes of at least one day's duration (Pope, 2006).

Employers, like General Motors, characterized the sit-downs as an affront to law and order and the property rights not only of corporations but of every homeowner, claiming that they were 'striking at the heart of the right of possession of private property' (Pope, 2006, p. 61). Indeed, in a very real sense, the sit down was a very direct challenge to dominant property tropes, including the presumptive territorial sovereignty of the owner. However, the sit-down can also be seen, like the squat, as articulating an alternative property claim threatened by the right to exclude. Pope (2006) notes the strategic use of property against the employer, based on the claim by workers that they had a collective property right in their labour, this being seen as a fundamental human right predicated on the need for survival. Unlike corporate property rights, the worker's property right concerned an asset that was essential to survival. 'Unfortunately in the past, the resources of the state have been too largely employed to protect, as against human property rights, an entirely different kind of property right – those of propertied classes', argued one unionist (quoted in Pope, 2006, p. 72). 'Human rights over property rights!'

was the slogan (71). Unionists rejected the analogy between corporate property rights and those of the homeowner. Corporate property in the factory, it was pointed out, was no castle because the exclusion of others would render it worthless. The 'corporation's property rights in the factory have value only as the worker's property right in the job is preserved and respected', noted one organizer, echoing Kelly's (2014) argument regarding the logical and practical absurdity of absolute exclusion. The right to exclude must be countered by the right not to be excluded.

However, the U.S. Supreme Court, in *Fansteel*,[3] ultimately ruled that sit-down strikes were illegal, arguing that the corporation's property right was essentially that of a person. While recognizing that employer's actions against unions could be reprehensible, the right to exclude of the former trumped the right not to be excluded of the latter. Despite this, sit-down strikes played a crucial role in the continuing struggle to democratize the workplace (Pope, 2006). Highly vulnerable workers continue to use them. Los Angeles Wal-Mart employees, frustrated at the refusal of the company to allow unionization, engaged in a sit-down strike in their store in November 2014, for example, placing tape over their mouths in protest at the company's attempts to silence workers who protested their pay and conditions (People's World Online, 2014).

Moreover, recent decisions have argued for an accommodation of the property rights of employers and the interests of workers in sit-down strikes, 'with as little destruction of one as is consistent with maintenance of the other'.[4] The U.S. National Labour Relations Board has developed a series of factors to be weighed, including the reason for the worker's occupation and its duration, as well as the degree to which the workers deprived the employer of access to property or attempted to 'seize' property[5].

The *Quietflex* criteria have been subsequently applied to a Wal-Mart labour dispute, which the dissenting judge characterizes as a 'modern sit-down strike'[6] in Richmond, California. Several workers engaged in a work stoppage at the store, occupying a small 'customer waiting area' near the front of the store, to protest a supervisor who

---

3 *NLRB v. Fansteel Metallurgical Corp.*, 306 U.S. 240 (1939), 1724
4 *Hudgens v. NLRB*, 424 U.S. 507, 522 (1976)
5 QuietflexMfg. Co., 344 NLRB 1055, 1056–1057, 2005)
6 Wal-Mart Stores Inc., 364 NLRB No. 118, 8

allegedly made racist and violent comments at an African-American employee and threatened to 'shoot the union'. While the National Labor Relations Board found in favour of the workers, a dissenting judge argued that the economic function of a retail establishment, designed so as to create a 'positive, carefully cultivated, in-store experience' (ibid. 11), had been compromised, and thus backed the owner's right.

Anti-racists

The right to exclude does not, of course, operate in a generalized fashion. Those who are proportionately subjected to the duties it generates rather than the benefits it affects are by definition those more marginalized within any society. As discussed previously, property's territory often serves to hold up forms of hegemonic whiteness, placing racialized people in spaces of vulnerability and violence. Under certain conditions, the racialization of property's territories becomes more sharply formalized, as in modern-day Stand Your Ground laws, as well as in the segregationist cities of the U.S. South. Black patrons in Greensboro, North Carolina were excluded from lunch counters in the 1960s through the use of local legal custom, i.e. the owners' private exercise of their common law right to exclude, Peñalver and Katyal (2007) note. This, in turn, echoed a highly territorialized set of property relations that had sustained slavery and subsequent forms of power and exclusion (Delaney, 1998).

Black students chose to break the territorial code by sitting at the counters and asking to be served. The sit-ins were immensely controversial, even amongst sympathizers, as they broke the dominant spatial grammar of race, power, property, and territory. Hundreds were arrested and charged with criminal trespass. New laws were passed to buttress the right to exclude. For many, civil rights activism was an affront to the territory of property. For President Harry Truman, '[i]f anyone came into my store and tried to stop business, I'd throw him out' (quoted in Peñalver & Katyal, 2007, p. 1118). Yet others noted that there was clearly tension here. The *Greensboro Daily News* editorialized that while property rights were sacred, there was an unfairness in inviting Black people into a business and then denying them the full use of that space.

These sit-ins proved a powerful catalyst for the emergent civil rights movement and set the stage for the U.S. Civil Rights Act of 1964, which prohibits discrimination on the basis of race in 'any place of

public accommodation', substantially curtailing the right of shop-
owners to exclude on whatever ground they see fit. As noted, Joseph
Singer (2000, p. 41) argues that this should not be thought of as pitting
the owner's property rights against the equality rights of the customer
but rather as a negotiation that is internal to property itself:

> Accommodations law not only limit the property rights of the
> owner, but transfer one of these rights to nonowners . . . The
> owner's right to exclude is limited by a competing public right of
> access to the property. A right of access to property possessed by
> another is a property right.

Houseless people

The houseless are those who are forced to experience only the exclusionary territorialization of private property without any compensa-
tory right to territory of their own. They live the 'Lockean hell' (Davis,
1991): not simply are they 'under the power of others – to be domi-
nated by them or dependent on them – in respect of where one may
be' (Essert, 2017, p. 266), but also, they must negotiate the legal reality
that 'that there is nowhere that [they] are in charge of, nowhere that
everyone else has no right to be without [their] leave' (279–280). As
Waldron (1991) notes, the spaces in which the houseless can exercise
their freedom, including fundamental freedoms such as the right to
sleep without being disturbed by others, are hedged in by the territory
of private property:

> For the most part the homeless are excluded from all of the places
> governed by private property rules, whereas the rest of us are, in
> the same sense, excluded from all but one (or maybe all but a few)
> of those places. That is another way of saying that each of us has
> at least one place to be in a country composed of private places,
> whereas the homeless person has none.
>
> (300)

The rules of private property are thus: for the houseless person, 'a series
of fences that stand between them and somewhere to be, somewhere
to act' (Waldron, 1991, p. 302). The only place a houseless person 'can
be', under prevailing property rules, is on public property in which, at
least in principle, the right not to be excluded is operative. The right,
however, has come under increased pressure, either directly – through

sweeps and bans – or indirectly, through the increased regulation of the behaviour of homeless people.

Under such conditions, it is not surprising that houseless people opt for congregate living through the creation of tent cities, in preference to the risks of solitary rough sleeping or the degradation of shelters. City authorities have often sought to displace tent cities, relying upon their right to exclude. In British Columbia, for example, municipal authorities have invoked their trespass powers in order to expel tent cities based on their title to the land.

Houseless people and their allies resist such territorial logics, however. A 2014 eviction order against a large tent city in Oppenheimer Park in downtown Vancouver was countered by an eviction against the City crafted by Indigenous protestors, who pointed out that many of the residents of the tent city were Indigenous and that the park itself was on unceded Indigenous land. As such, the homeless were said to have the right not to be excluded; in other words[7]:

> We, the indigenous people here today in Oppenheimer Park, do hereby assert our Aboriginal Title. . . . Our people have held title to this land since time immemorial, and we are exerting our right to exclusive authority, recognized as an inherent element of our title, over this land and this camp. . . . We now require that you leave this place and cease any attempts to remove people or their belongings from this place.
>
> (CBC News Online, 2014)

This counter-claim, unsurprisingly, was of more rhetorical than practical force. Yet, the courts have sometimes been reluctant to enforce

---

7 Oppenheimer Park, the location for the encampment, is layered with struggles against exclusion, many of which continue to resonate. Named after a former City mayor who was a land speculator in 1880, the park is on the traditional territory of Musqueam and Squamish First Nations. The territorial grid that created the park, sustained by state violence, displaced them from their traditional territory, although as is evident, they continue to assert title and sovereignty. The park holds an annual Japanese-Canadian festival, located here as the surrounding neighbourhood was the home to a large Japanese-Canadian community, forcibly removed, with their property liquidated, in the 1940s. Importantly, the festival organizers, in an act of solidarity with the tent city, elected to move the festival in 2014, and opposed the removal of the tent city. The park is also a site closely affiliated with labour organizing in the earlier years of the century, including a gathering in 1912 involving the International Workers of the World, who were forced to use the park because of the violence visited upon them when they attempted to organize at the private worksite.

the City's right to exclude in relation to such encampments. For example, a tent city was established in the city of Victoria, Canada, on state-owned land outside the courthouse. The state sought an interlocutory injunction (i.e. a court order compelling or preventing a party from certain actions pending final determination of a case) requiring the ejection of the encampment, based in part on the state's rights as land owner. The state argued that the case did not require the use of a prevailing test that weighed the 'balance of convenience' (that is, the interests of both parties), arguing that 'once they [owners] have shown that their property rights are being wrongfully interfered with, and the defendants continue to commit the wrong, they have established their entitlement to an injunction'.[8]

However, Chief Justice Hinkson rejected the state's slam-dunk Blackstonean argument, insisting on the need to weigh the property interests of the state with those of the residents of the encampment. Expressing a refreshingly cautious evaluation of the state's arguments regarding the health, safety, and fire risks of the tent city, he cited several countervailing benefits were it to continue. Encampment residents, he noted, seemed healthier, were better able to access services, were physically safer, were able to better secure their personal property, and enjoyed a heightened sense of community. Conversely, the alternative spaces to which they could go were deemed limited (the number of shelter beds was insufficient) and often problematic, quoting one resident who noted that '[s]helters make people feel less than. We already feel less than'.[9] In conclusion, Hinkson found that:

> the balance of convenience is overwhelmingly in favour of the defendants, who simply have nowhere to move to, if the injunction were to issue, other than shelters that are incapable of meeting the needs of some of them, or will result in their constant disruption and a perpetuation of a relentless series of daily moves to the streets, doorways, and parks of the City of Victoria.[10]

8 *British Columbia v. Adamson* 2016 BCSC 584, §23)
9 *British Columbia v Adamson*, § 169
10 *British Columbia v Adamson*, § 184

The state's right to exclude, put another way, needed to reckon with the right of the houseless not to be excluded.

Reterritorializing property

Many of the struggles noted previously challenge hegemonic forms yet also reinscribe certain characteristics of the ownership model. Struggles against dispossession and for land rights 'are persistently coopted into the language of possession' (Porter, 2014, p. 395), failing to 'unsettle the colonial conceit of proper and propertied human subjectivity' (Butler & Athanasiou, 2013, p. 27). As a result, struggles 'that focus on securing property rights run the risk of reinvigorating the racial property regime rather than undermining it' (Dorries, 2022, p. 311; Nichols, 2018). Yet there are powerfully counter-hegemonic contestations that take us to a space 'without property' (Dorries, 2022) in compelling ways.

Indigenous ontologies, in particular, offer an alternative reading, challenging the logic of severability (Blomley, 2011) that is central to the ownership model. Rather than imagining land as a discrete object that can be acted upon by autonomous subjects driven by desire and domination, land is conceived as entangled in life-giving relations, obligations, and duties with the human and more-than-human world (Dorries, 2022), constituting a form of 'grounded normativity' based on on-going right relations that take us beyond colonial private property. As Simpson puts it, 'Indigenous bodies don't relate to the land by possessing, owning, or having control over it. We relate to land through connection – generative, affirmative, complex, overlapping, and non-linear relationship' (2017, p. 43). As such, the solution to dispossession is not possession, she argues, but 'deep, reciprocal, consensual attachment' (43).

Indigenous ontologies also offer an alternative understanding of territory. Lenape scholar Joanne Barker (2018) notes the way in which her Nation's territory has been systematically eroded through debt relations. She draws from the work of Park (2016), who documents the manner in which the recovery of debt through the forced sale or seizure of land is a seventeenth-century colonial innovation, departing from English practices, which made it very hard to remove families from their ancestral land. Conversely, in the Americas, debt relations became an instrument of colonial dispossession, reliant on Indigenous territorial seizure. Albeit eroded, Lenape territory becomes a counter analytic for Barker (2018). By this, she means that radical politics of land in settler societies need to reckon with the foundational seizure of Indigenous territory. But importantly, she also offers a different epistemology of territory. She rejects the idea of Lenape territory as a space of capitalist, settler property. Rather, she characterizes Lenape territory as 'a mode of relationality and related set of ethics and protocols for lived social responsibilities and governance defined within discrete Indigenous epistemologies' (Barker 2018, p. 21). If territory is a relational device, these relations work differently in Lenape territory, in other words. As Indigenous territory offers a different 'pedagogy of political movements and the frameworks of critical theory' (Barker, 2018, p. 20), so it provides lessons in the 'radical acts of imagining' (Bhandar, 2018, p. 200) required for the transformation of property.

We can also learn from related territorial struggles, such as those of the Landless Rural Workers' Movement (MST) in Brazil, heavily influenced by Indigenous and Black communities. In the Brazilian context, 'territory' is understood as the 'appropriation of space for political projects' (Halvorsen, 2018, p. 791) and is thus framed according to the rights of Indigenous peoples and Quilombola communities (rural communities of the Afro-descendants of former slaves). As a result, land is framed according to the maintenance and construction of social and political identities. Land access is not only framed according to economic well-being but also self-determination, emancipation, and collective life, reworking relations to land that go beyond property, narrowly defined:

> The struggles, achievements and access to land are crucial social processes that create territory, highlighting a relationship with land as beyond a means and place of production. They involve subjects who claim rights that transcend notions of private property. . . [moving beyond] a 'legal monoculture' of property law to socio-biodiverse practices of cultural accesses, uses, controls and tenures of land, leading to self-determination and to the constitution of rights to land and territories of life in Brazil.
>
> (Sauer & de Castro, 2020, p. 126)

Indigenous struggles against colonial dispossession should not be seen simply as a protest or even as an attempt to modify dominant property norms, therefore. Rather, they can also be read as a challenge to the monopoly of colonial law itself (McCreary, 2020, p. 126). Indigenous people may draw from a legal system predicated on obligations to territory in which land is framed as a 'place for life' (Sauer & de Castro, 2020, p. 117). Witsuwit'en hereditary chiefs who lead traditional matrilineal kinship groups called houses or *yikh* have blocked a proposed liquefied natural gas pipeline project running through their traditional territory in northwestern British Columbia for several years. The hereditary chiefs claim territorial jurisdiction under Witsuwit'en law, having never ceded title to the colonial state. Ownership and jurisdiction align in Witsuwit'en law. As Chief Delgamuukw argued before the Canadian courts,

> For us, the ownership of the territory is a marriage of the chief and the land. Each chief has an ancestor who encountered and acknowledged the life of the land. From such encounters come power. . . . This is the basis of our law.
>
> (quoted in McCreary, forthcoming, 77)

Settler colonial logics deny Indigenous sovereignty and law in order to assert territorial control. Colonial dispossession relies on a characterization of Indigenous people as nomadic and transitory, and incapable of law, with one judge characterizing precontact Witsuwit'en life as, at best, 'nasty, brutish and short'.[11] In an embodied enactment of Indigenous legal geography, Witsuwit'en hereditary chiefs created the Unist'ot'en Camp in 2010, placed on the proposed path of the pipeline, as 'a site of Witsuwit'en resurgence that enunciated a distinct paradigm for the conduct of lawful relations' (McCreary & Turner, 2018, p. 224). The Camp, and the regulation of territorial access conducted at the site, can thus be understood not only as a counter to dominant territorialized conceptions of title and sovereignty but also as an 'unambiguous embodiment of a present Indigenous territorial responsibility' (McCreary & Turner, 2018, p. 231).

We all 'take up space' and need 'sum room', as Sam Wallman's comic about land reminds us. The terms under which we take up space, clearly, are deeply consequential. Territory is a vital sociopolitical resource that shapes the ways in which we occupy space by organizing relations of access, presence, and use. A Western property system provides one legal framework that governs such territorial rules. But it is clearly not the only one, Chief Delgamuukw reminds us. Territory and law can be

---

11 *Delgamuukw v. British Columbia*, 1991 CanLII 2372 (BC SC) p. 21

differently configured. Yet the possibility of such alternatives is hedged in by hegemonic territorializations of property.

Such dominant geographies must be opened to scrutiny. Property is one crucial means by which we relate to land and to others. However, if it is constituted as a hard territory from which others are to be excluded, the solutions central to cohabitation with others on a finite and vulnerable planet become harder to attain. It becomes conceptually possible to parse dense, storied social spaces into segmented, extractable, and fungible units, emptying land into 'vacant lots' and 'parcels' (Graham, 2011). The possibilities of just relationships between settlers and Indigenous people are boxed into a zero-sum discourse centred on private property rights, castles, and white privilege. Alternatives that recognize that we all access land in and through relations with others, including nonhumans, become conceptually unavailable to us. Alternative spatial metaphors of networked reciprocity and entangled obligation are overwritten by the bright lines of fee simple property rights. Metaphoric spaces of dialogue are foreclosed as '[t]he' notion of common ground, the idea of shared values, is entirely obliterated by the dualist command of the fence' (Hayes, 2020, p. 333).

Yet property and territory can and should be reimagined. Property can open itself up to shared rather than individual entitlements, obligations rather than rights, collective imaginaries rather than private narratives. So too, territory can be conceived of differently – as a valued place rather than a redoubt, a door rather than a wall, and a zone of encounter rather than a line of expulsion.

To understand law, including property law, it is helpful to recognize the territory of property. Territory makes a difference, I have argued. It is not just a surface upon which law is performed. Rather than thinking of territory as obvious and given or as a 'natural' phenomenon, it is both a social product and a particular technology that organizes social relations in particular and consequential ways. When we encounter property in land, it is likely through its territorial manifestations. Property relations, therefore, are often experienced, judged, enacted, and contested in and through these territorial encounters. Territory, however, is not just an outcome of property law, however. It does important work in communicating, enforcing, legitimating, and complicating the relationality of property. For this and many other reasons, the territory of property needs to be queried and explored.

HOW DOES THIS LOOK TO SOMEONE ELSE?

WHO HAS THE KEYS?

WHAT WAS HERE B4?

Figure 6.2 'How does this look to someone else?'.

Source: From sobelow.org; reproduced with permission.

References

Agnew, J. (2009). Territory. In D. Gregory et al. (Eds.), *Dictionary of human geography* (pp. 746–747). Oxford: Blackwell.

Alexander, G. (1997). *Commodity and propriety: Competing visions of property in American legal thought, 1776–1970*. Chicago, IL: University of Chicago Press.

Alexander, G., & Peñalver, E. (Eds.). (2012). *An introduction to property theory*. Cambridge: Cambridge University Press.

Andreucci, D., García-Lamarca, M., Wedekind, J., & Swyngedouw, E. (2017). 'Value Grabbing': A political ecology of rent. *Capitalism Nature Socialism, 28*(3), 28–47.

Anonymous. (1994). Distributive liberty: A relational model of freedom, coercion, and property law. *Harvard Law Review, 107*(4), 859–876.

Ardrey, R. (1966). *The territorial imperative*. New York: Atheneum.

Atkinson, R., & Blandy, S. (2017). *Domestic fortress: Fear and the new home front*. Manchester: University of Manchester Press.

Aylmer, G. E. (1980). The meaning and definition of 'property' in seventeenth century England. *Past and Present, 86*, 87–97.

Babie, P. (2013). The spatial: A forgotten dimension of property. *San Diego Law Review, 50*(323).

Baker, J. H. (1971). *An introduction to English legal history*. London: Butterworths.

Banner, S. (1999). Two properties, one land: Law and space in nineteenth century New Zealand. *Law and Social Inquiry, 24*(4), 807–852.

Barker, J. (2018). Territory as analytic: The dispossession of Lenapehoking and the subprime crisis. *Social Text, 36*(2), 19–39.

Begg, M. (2007). *Legislating British Columbia: A history of BC land law, 1858–1978*. Masters of Laws thesis, University of British Columbia.

Bell, V. (2019). The white to bear arms: How immunity provisions in stand your ground statutes lead to an unequal application of the law for black gun owners. *Fordham Urban Law Journal, 46*(4), 902–941.

Bending, S., & McRae, A. (Eds.). (2003). *The writing of rural England 1500–1800*. Basingstoke: Springer.

Bennett, J. A. (1991). Geometry and surveying in early-seventeenth century England. *Annals of Science, 48*(4), 345–354.

Bentham, J. (1999). Security and equality of property. In C. B. Macpherson (Ed.), *Property: Mainstream and critical positions* (pp. 41–58). Toronto: University of Toronto Press. (Original work published 1830)

Benton, L. (2010). *A search for sovereignty: Law and geography in European empires, 1400–1900*. New York: Cambridge University Press.

Beresford, M. (1998). *History on the ground*. Stroud: Sutton Publishing.

Berger, B. (2021). *Property to race/race to property*. Unpublished paper. https://papers.ssrn.com/sol3/papers.cfm?abstract_id=3825124,

Best, A., & Ramirez, M. M. (2021). Urban specters. *Environment and Planning D: Society and Space, 39*(6), 1043–1054.

Bhandar, B. (2018). *Colonial lives of property: Law, land, and racial regimes of ownership*. Durham, NC: Duke University Press.

Blackhawk, N. (2006). *Violence over the land: Indians and Empire in the early American West*. Cambridge: Harvard University Press.

Blackmar, E. (1989). *Manhattan for rent*. Ithaca, NY: Cornell University Press.

Blackstone, W. (1979a). *Commentaries on the laws of England: Of the rights of things* (Vol. 2). Chicago, IL: University of Chicago Press. (Original work published 1766)

Blackstone, W. (1979b). *Commentaries on the laws of England: Of private wrongs* (Vol. 3). Chicago, IL: University of Chicago Press. (Original work published 1768)

Blackstone, W. (1979c). *Commentaries on the laws of England: Of public wrongs* (Vol. 4). Chicago, IL: University of Chicago Press. (Original work published 1769)

Blith, W. (1652). *The English improver improved or the survey of husbandry surveyed discovering the improveableness of all lands*. London.

Blomley, N. (2003). Law, property, and the spaces of violence: The frontier, the survey, and the grid. *Annals, Association of American Geographers, 93*(1), 121–141.

Blomley, N. (2004). *Unsettling the city: Urban land and the politics of property*. New York: Routledge.

Blomley, N. (2005). The borrowed view: Privacy, propriety, and the entanglements of property. *Law and Social Inquiry, 30*(4), 617–661.

Blomley, N. (2007). Making private property: Enclosure, common right, and the work of hedges. *Rural History, 18*(1), 1–21.

Blomley, N. (2009). Homelessness, rights and the delusions of property. *Urban Geography, 30*(6), 577–590.

Blomley, N. (2011). Cuts, flows, and the geographies of property. *Law, Culture and the Humanities, 7*, 203–216.

Blomley, N. (2013). Performing property, making the world. *Canadian Journal of Law and Jurisprudence, 26*(1), 23–48.

Blomley, N. (2014). Disentangling property, performing space. In R. Rose-Redwood & M. Glass (Eds.), *Performativity, politics, and the production of social space*. New York: Routledge.

Blomley, N. (2015). The ties that blind: Making fee simple in the British Columbia treaty process. *Transactions of the Institute of British Geographers, 40*(2), 168–179.

Blomley, N. (2016a). The territory of property. *Progress in Human Geography, 40*(5), 593–609.

Blomley, N. (2016b). The boundaries of property: Complexity, relationality, spatiality. *Law and Society Review, 50*(1), 224–255.

Blomley, N. (2016c). The right to not be excluded: Common property and the right to stay put. In A. Amin & P. Howell (Eds.), *Releasing the commons: Rethinking the futures of the commons* (pp. 89–106). New York: Routledge.

Blomley, N. (2020a). Precarious territory: Property law, housing and the social order. *Antipode, 52*(1), 26–57.

Blomley, N. (2020b). Urban commoning and the right not to be excluded. In D. Ozkan & G. B. Buyuksarac (Eds.), *Commoning the city* (pp. 89–103). New York: Routledge.

Blomley, N., Flynn, A., & Sylvestre, M.-E. (2020c). Governing the possessions of the precariously housed: A critical legal geography. *Annual Review of Law and Social Science, 16*, 165–181.

Blomley, N., & The Right to Remain Collective. (2021). Making property outlaws: Law and relegation. *International Journal of Urban and Regional Research, 45*(6), 911–929.

Brighenti, A. M. (2006). On territory as relationship and law as territory. *Canadian Journal of Law and Society, 21*(2), 65–86.

Brighenti, A. M. (2010a). On territorology: Towards a general science of territory. *Theory, Culture & Society, 27*(1), 52–72.

Brighenti, A. M. (2010b). Lines, barred lines: Movement, territory and the law. *International Journal of Law in Context, 6*(3), 217–227.

Bromley, D. W. (1998). Rousseau's revenge: The Demise of the Freehold Estate. In H. M. Jacobs (Ed.), *Who owns America? Social conflict over property rights* (pp. 19–28). Madison, WI: University of Wisconsin Press.

Brückner, M., & Poole, K. (2002). The plot thickens: Surveying manuals, drama, and the materiality of narrative form in early modern England. *ELH, 69*(3), 617–648.

Butler, J., & Athanasiou, A. (2013). *Dispossession: The performative in the political.* Cambridge: Polity Press.

Byrd, J. A., Goldstein, A., Melamed, J., & Reddy, C. (2018). Predatory value: Economies of dispossession and disturbed relationalities. *Social Text, 36*(2), 1–18.

Canny, N. P. (1973). The ideology of English colonization: From Ireland to America. *William and Mary Quarterly, 30*, 575–98.

CBC News Online. (2014). Oppenheimer homeless camp: First nations members issue eviction notice to Vancouver. *CBC News Online.* www.cbc.ca/news/canada/british-columbia/oppenheimer-homeless-camp-first-nations-membersissue-eviction-notice-to-vancouver-1.2712736

Christophers, B. (2018). *The new enclosure.* London: Verso.

Churchill, W. (2013). *The people's rights.* New York: Rosetta Books. (Original work published 1910)

Coalition to Stop Gun Violence. (2021). *Stand your ground laws increase gun violence and perpetuate racial disparities.* csgv.org.

Cockburn, P. (2018). *The politics of dependence: Economic parasites and vulnerable lives.* London: Springer.

Cohen, F. (1954). Dialogue on private property. *Rutgers Law Review, 9*, 357.

Cohen, M. (1927). Property and sovereignty. *Cornell Law Quarterly, 13*(1), 8–30.

Cooper, D. (2007). Opening up ownership: Community belonging, belongings, and the productive life of property. *Law and Social Inquiry, 32*(3), 625–664.

Cosgrove, D. (1985). Prospect, perspective, and the evolution of the landscape idea. *Transactions of the Institute of British Geographers, 10*(1), 45–62.

Cresswell, T. (1996). *In place/out of place: Geography, ideology and transgression*. Minneapolis, MN: University of Minnesota Press.

Cronon, W. (2003). *Changes on the land: Indians, colonists, and the ecology of New England*. New York: Hill & Wang.

Crosby, A. W. (1997). *The measure of reality: Quantification and western society, 1250–1600*. Cambridge: Cambridge University Press.

D'Adda, G., Delgado, L., & Sala, E. (2018). Responding to the precarization of housing: A case study of PAH Barcelona. In H. Carr, B. Edgeworth, & C. Hunter (Eds.), *Law and the precarious home: Socio-legal perspectives on the home in insecure times* (pp. 289–315). Oxford: Hart.

Dagan, H. (2021). *A liberal theory of property*. Cambridge: Cambridge University Press.

Dahlman, C. (2009). Territory. In C. Gallaher, C. T. Dahlman, M. Gilmartin, A. Mountz, & P. Shirlow (Eds.), *Key concepts in political geography*. Los Angeles, CA: SAGE.

David, D., & Shoked, N. (2019). Private property's edges. *Boston College Law Review, 60*, 753.

Davies, M. (2007). *Property: Meanings, histories, theories*. Abingdon: Routledge-Cavendish.

Davis, M. (1991). Afterword a logic like hell's: Being homeless in Los Angeles. *UCLA Law Review, 39*(1), 325–332.

Delaney, D. (1998). *Race, place, and the law, 1836–1948*. Austin, TX: University of Texas Press.

Delaney, D. (2005). *Territory: A short introduction*. Malden, MA: Blackwell.

Delaney, D. (2010). *The spatial, the legal, and the pragmatics of world-making: Nomospheric investigations*. New York: Routledge.

Delano-Smith, C., & Kain, R. J. P. (1999). *English maps: A history*. Toronto: University of Toronto Press.

Depoorter, B. (2011). Fair trespass. *Columbia Law Review, 111*, 1090–1135.

Desmond, M. (2016). *Evicted: Poverty and profit in the American city*. New York: Crown Publishers.

Dirlam, J., Steidley, T., & Jacobs, D. (2021). A link to the past: Race, lynchings, and the passage of stand-your-ground laws. *The Sociological Quarterly, 62*(4), 690–711.

Dorries, H. (2022). What is planning without property? Relational practices of being and belonging. *Environment and Planning D, Society & Space, 40*(2), 306–318.

Elden, S. (2005). Missing the point: Globalization, deterritorialization and the space of the world. *Transactions of the Institute of British Geographers, 30*(1), 8–19.

Elden, S. (2010). Land, terrain, territory. *Progress in Human Geography, 34*(6), 799–817.

Elden, S. (2013). *The birth of territory*. Chicago, IL: University of Chicago Press.

Elden, S. (2021). Terrain, politics, history. *Dialogues in Human Geography*, *1*(2), 170–189.

Ellickson, R. C. (1993). Property in land. *Yale Law Journal*, *102*(6), 1315–1400.

Essert, C. (2017). Property and homelessness. *Philosophy and Public Affairs*, *44*(4), 266–295.

Fanon, F. (1963). *The wretched of the earth*. New York: Grove Press.

Ferencz, S., Flynn, A., Blomley, N., & Sylvestre, M.-E. (forthcoming). Are tents a 'home'? Extending section 8 privacy rights for the precariously housed. *McGill Law Journal*.

Fields, G. (2017). *Enclosure: Palestinian landscapes in a historical mirror*. Oakland, CA: University of California Press.

Fisher, D. (2016). Freeze-framing territory: Time and its significance in land governance. *Space and Polity*, *20*(2), 212–225.

Flynn, A., & Wagner, E. (2020). A colonial castle: Defence of property in R v Stanley. *Canadian Bar Review*, *98*(2), 358–387.

Freeman, L., & Blomley, N. (2019). Enacting property: Making space for the public in the municipal library. *EPC: Politics and Space*, *37*(2), 199–218.

Gazit, N. (2015). State-sponsored Vigilantism: Jewish Settlers' violence in the occupied Palestinian territories. *Sociology*, *49*(3), 438–454.

Graham, N. (2011). *Lawscape: Property, environment, law*. Oxford: Routledge.

Gray, K., & Gray, S. (2009). *Elements of land law* (5th ed.). Oxford: Oxford University Press.

Gurney, C. M. (1999). Lowering the drawbridge: A case study of analogy and metaphor in the social construction of home-ownership. *Urban Studies*, *36*(10), 1705–1722.

Hafetz, J. L. (2002). 'A man's home is his castle?': Reflections on the home, the family, and privacy during the late nineteenth and early twentieth centuries. *William and Mary Journal of Women and the Law*, *8*, 175–242.

Hale, R. L. (1943). Bargaining, duress, and economic liberty. *Columbia Law Review*, *43*(5).

Hall, D. (2013). *Land*. Cambridge: Polity Press.

Hallowell, A. I. (1943). The nature and function of property as a social institution. *Journal of Legal and Political Sociology*, *1*, 115–138.

Halvorsen, S. (2018). Decolonising territory: Dialogues with Latin American knowledges and grassroots strategies. *Progress in Human Geography*, *43*(5), 790–814.

Harris, C. (1993). Whiteness as property. *Harvard Law Review*, *106*(8), 1707–1791.

Harris, C. (2002). *Making native space: Colonialism, resistance, and reserves in British Columbia*. Vancouver: UBC Press.

Harris, C. (2003). *Making Native space: Colonialism, resistance, and reserves in British Columbia*. Vancouver: UBC Press.

Harris, C. (2020). *A bounded land*. Vancouver: UBC Press.

Hartlib, S. (1653). *A discoverie for division or setting out of land. . . .* London: Printed for Richard Wodenothe.

Harvey, D. (1974). Class-monopoly rent, finance capital and the urban revolution. *Regional Studies*, *8*(3–4), 239.

Harvey, P. D. A. (1993). *Maps in Tudor England*. Chicago, IL: University of Chicago Press.

Hayes, N. (2020). *The book of trespass: Crossing the lines that divide us*. London: Bloomsbury Circus.

Hohfeld, W. (1913). Some fundamental legal conceptions as applied in judicial reasoning. *The Yale Law Journal, 23*(1), 16–59.

Homes Not Jails (2013). *It's vacant. Take it!*. Copy with author. Online pamphlet/zine.

Ingold, T. (1987). Territoriality and tenure: The appropriation of space in hunting and gathering societies. In T. Ingold (Ed.), *The appropriation of nature: Essays on human ecology and social relations* (pp. 130–164). Iowa City, IA: University of Iowa Press.

Inwood, J. F. J., & Bonds, A. (2017). Property and whiteness: the Oregon standoff and the contradictions of the U.S. Settler State. *Space and Polity, 21*(3), 253–268.

Johnston, S. (1991). Mathematical practitioners and instruments in Elizabethan England. *Annals of Science, 48,* 319–344.

Joshua, F., Inwood, J., & Bonds, A. (2017). Property and whiteness: The Oregon standoff and the contradictions of the U.S. Settler State. *Space and Polity, 21*(3), 253–268.

Keenan, S. (2015). *Subversive property: Law and the production of spaces of belonging*. New York: Routledge.

Kelly, D. B. (2014). The right to include. *Emory Law Journal, 63,* 857–924.

Kennedy, D. (1991). The stakes of law, or, Hale and Foucault. *Legal Studies Forum, 15*(4), 327–365.

King, P. (1989). Farmers and the failure of legal sanctions in England 1750–1850. *Past & Present, 125,* 116–150.

Kitchin, R., & Dodge, M. (2007). Rethinking maps. *Progress in Human Geography, 31*(3), 331–344.

Krueckeberg, D. A. (1999). The grapes of rent: A history of renting in a country of owners. *Housing Policy Debate, 10*(1), 9–30.

Lancione, M. (2020). Radical housing: On the politics of dwelling as difference. *International Journal of Housing Policy, 20*(2), 273–289.

Li, T. M. (2014). What is land? Assembling a resource for global investment. *Transactions of the Institute of British Geographers, 39,* 589–602.

Light, C. (2015). From a duty to retreat to stand your ground: The race and gender politics of do-it-yourself-defense. *Cultural Studies: Critical Methodologies, 15*(4), 292.

Linklater, A. (2013). *Owning the earth: The transforming history of land ownership*. New York: Bloomsbury.

Locke, J. (1980). *Second treatise of government*. Indianapolis, IN: Hackett. (Original work published 1690)

Love, J. (1687). *Geodæsie: Or the art of surveying and measuring of land made easie*. London: John Taylor. (Original work published 1623)

Macpherson, C. B. (1962). *The political theory of possessive individualism: Hobbes to Locke*. Oxford: Oxford University Press.

Manning, R. B. (1988). *Village revolts: Social protest and popular disturbances in England, 1509–1640*. Oxford: Clarendon Press.

McCarthy, S. D. (2014). Squatting: Lifting the heavy burden to evict unwanted company. *University of Massachusetts Law Review, 9*(2), 156–192.

McClain, L. (1995). Inviolability and privacy: The castle, the sanctuary and the body. *Yale Journal of Law and the Humanities, 7*(2), 195–242.

McCreary, T. (2020). Between the commodity and the gift: The Coastal GasLink pipeline and the contested temporalities of Canadian and Witsuwit'en law. *Journal of Human Rights and the Environment, 11*, 122–145.

McCreary, T. (forthcoming). *Indigenous legalities, pipeline viscosities*. Edmonton: University of Alberta Press.

McCreary, T., & Turner, J. (2018). The contested scales of indigenous and settler jurisdiction: Unist'ot'en struggles with Canadian pipeline governance. *Studies in Political Economy, 99*(3), 223–245.

McDonagh, B. (2009). Subverting the ground: Private property and public protest in the sixteenth-century Yorkshire Wolds. *Agricultural History Review, 57*(2), 191–206.

McDonagh, B. (2013). Making and breaking property: Negotiating enclosure and common rights in sixteenth-century England. *History Workshop Journal, 76*, 32–56.

McDonagh, B., & Griffin, C. (2016). Occupy! Historical geographies of property, protest and the commons. *Journal of Historical Geography, 53*, 1–10.

McRae, A. (1993). To know one's own: Estate surveying and the representation of the land in early modern England. *The Huntington Library Quarterly, 56*(4), 333–357.

McRae, A. (1996). *God speed the plough: The representation of Agrarian England, 1500–1660*. Cambridge: Cambridge University Press.

Merrill, T. W. (1998). Property and the right to exclude. *Nebraska Law Review, 77*, 730–754.

Merrill, T. W., & Smith, H. E. (2007). The morality of property. *William and Mary Law Review, 481*, 1849–1895.

Mitchell, J. H. (2015). *Trespassing: An inquiry into the private ownership of lands*. Hanover: University Press of New England.

Mitchell, T. (1995). *Colonizing Egypt*. Berkeley, CA: University of California Press.

Moore, A. (1653). *Bread for the poor and advancement of the English Nation promised by enclosure of the wastes and common grounds of England*. London.

Nedelsky, J. (1989). Reconceiving autonomy: Some thoughts and possibilities. *Yale Journal of Law and Feminism, 1*(6), 36.

Nedelsky, J. (1990). Law, boundaries and the bounded self. *Representations, 30*, 162–189.

Neeson, J. M. (1993). *Commoners: Common right, enclosure, and social change in England, 1700–1820*. Cambridge: Cambridge University Press.

Neuwirth, R. (2005). *Shadow cities: A billion cities, a new urban world*. New York: Routledge.

Nichols, R. (2018). Theft is property! The recursive logic of dispossession. *Political Theory, 46*(1), 3–28.

Norden, J. (1979). *The surveiors dialogue*. Norwood, NJ: Theatrum Orbis Terrarum/ Walter J Johnson. (Original work published 1618)

Overton, M. (1996). *Agricultural revolution in England: The transformation of the Agrarian economy 1500–1850*. Cambridge: Cambridge University Press.

Paasi, A., Md Ferdoush, A., Jones, R., Murphy, A., Agnew, J., Espejo, P. O., Fall, J. J., & Peterle, G. (2022). Locating the territoriality of territory in border studies. *Political Geography, 95*. https://doi.org/10.1016/j.polgeo.2021.102584.

Page, J. (2021). *Public property, law and society*. New York: Routledge.

Painter, J. (2010). Rethinking territory. *Antipode, 42*(5), 1090–1118.

Park, K-S. (2016). Money, mortgages, and the conquest of America. *Law and Social Inquiry, 41*(4), 1006–1035.

Pasternak, S. (2017). *Grounded authority: The Algonquins of Barriere Lake against the state*. Minneapolis, MN: University of Minnesota Press.

Peluso, N. (1996). Fruit trees and family trees in an anthropogenic forest: Ethics of access, property zones, and environmental change in Indonesia. *Comparative Studies in Society and History, 38*(3).

Peñalver, E. (2005). Property as entrance. *Virginia Law Review, 91*(8), 1889–1972.

Peñalver, E. M., & Katyal S. K. (2007). Property outlaws. *University of Pennsylvania Law Review, 155*, 1095–1186.

People's World Online. (2014, November 13). Walmart workers begin first in-store sitdown strike in company history. *People's World Online*. www.peoplesworld. org/article/walmart-workers-begin-first-in-store-sitdown-strike-in-company-history/.

Pipes, R. (1999). *Property and freedom*. New York: Vintage.

Pope, J. (2006). Lawmaking, sit-down strikes, and the shaping of American industrial relations, 1935–1958. *Law and History Review, 24*(1), 45–113.

Porter, L. (2014). Possessory politics and the conceit of procedure: Exposing the cost of rights under conditions of dispossession. *Planning Theory, 13*(4), 387–406.

Pottage, A. (1994). The measure of land. *The Modern Law Review, 57*(3), 361–384.

Powell, J., & Webster, G. C. (1994). Geography, ethnogeography, and the perspective of the Kwakwaka'wakw. In R. Galois (Ed.), *Kwakwaka'wakw Settlements, 1775–1920: A geographical analysis and gazetteer* (pp. 4–11). Vancouver: UBC Press.

Rackham, O. (1986). *The history of the English countryside*. London: J.M. Dent and Sons, Ltd.

Raibmon, P. (2008). Unmaking native space. In A. Harmon & J. Borrows (Eds.), *The power of promises: Rethinking Indian treaties in the Pacific Northwest* (pp. 56–85). Seattle, WA: University of Washington Press.

Reich, C. (1964). The new property. *Yale Law Journal, 73*, 733–787.

Robertson, M. (1995). Property and ideology. *Canadian Journal of Law and Jurisprudence, 8*(2), 275–296.

Rose, C. (1994). *Property and persuasion: Essays in the history, theory, and rhetoric of ownership*. Boulder, CO: Westview Press.

Ross, A. (2011). Improvement on the grant estates in Strathspey in the later eighteenth century: Theory, practice, and failure? In Hoyle (Ed.), *Custom, improvement, and the landscape* (pp. 289–311). New York: Routledge.

Rowbotham, P. (1978). *Trespass law and territoriality: A geographic and evolutionary perspective*. PhD thesis, SFU Geography.

Roy, A. (2017). Dis/possessive collectivism: Property and personhood at city's end. *Geoforum, 80*, A1–A11.

Russell-Brown, K. (2015). Go ahead and shoot: The law might have your back. In D. Johnson, A. Farrell, & P. Y. Warren (Eds.), *Deadly injustice: Trayvon Martin, race, and the criminal justice system* (pp. 115–144). New York: New York University Press.

Sack, R. D. (1983). Human territoriality: A theory. *Annals of the Association of American Geographers, 73*(1), 55–74.

Sack, R. D. (1986). *Human territoriality: Its theory and history*. Cambridge: Cambridge University Press.

Saito, N. T. (2015). Race and decolonization: Whiteness as property in the American settler colonial project. *Harvard Journal on Racial and Ethnic Justice, 31*, 31–63.

Sampson, M. (1990). 'Property' in seventeenth century English political thought. In G. J. Schochet, P. E. Tatspaugh, & C. Brobeck (Eds.), *Religion, resistance and civil war: Papers presented at the Folger Institute Seminar*, Washington DC: Folger Institute (pp. 259–275).

Sauer, S., & de Castro, L. F. P. (2020). Land and territory: Struggles for land and territorial rights in Brazil. In O. De Schutter & B. Rajagopal (Eds.), *Property rights from below: Commodification of land and the counter-movement* (pp. 113–130). London: Routledge.

Seipp, D. (1994). The concept of property in early common law. *Law and History Review, 12*(1), 29–91.

Seipp, D. (1996). The distinction between crime and tort in the early common law. *Boston University Law Review, 76*, 59–88.

Shakesheff, T. (2002). Wood and crop theft in rural Herefordshire, 1800–60. *Rural History, 13*, 1–17.

Shehadeh, R. (2008). *Palestinian walks: Forays into a vanishing landscape*. New York: Scribner.

Shrubsole, G. (2019). *Who owns England?* London: William Collins.

Simpson, A. W. B. (1986). *A history of the land law* (2nd ed.). Oxford: Clarendon Press.

Simpson, L. B. (2017). *As we have always done*. Minneapolis, MN: University of Minnesota Press.

Singer, A. (2021). *Ahmaud Arbery's suspects' trial defense taps a racist legal legacy*. www.nbcnews.com/think/opinion/ahmaud-arbery-suspects-trial-defense-taps-racist-legal-legacy-ncna1283274.

Singer, J. (1991). Sovereignty and property. *Northwestern University Law Review, 86*(1), 1.

Singer, J. (2000). *Entitlement: The paradoxes of property*. New Haven, CT: Yale University Press.

Singer, J. (2008). Things that we would like to take for granted: Mimimum standards for the legal framework for a free and democratic society. *Harvard Law and Policy Review, 139*(2), 139–159.

Singer, J. (2015). We don't serve your kind here: Public accommodations and the mark of Sodom. *Boston University Law Review, 95*, 929–950.

Singer, J. W. (2006). The ownership society and takings of property: Castles, investments, and just obligations. *Harvard Environmental Law Review, 30*, 309–338.

Slack, P. (2015). *The invention of improvement: Information and material progress in Seventeenth Century England.* Oxford: Oxford University Press.

Smail, D. L. (1999). *Imaginary cartographies: Possession and identity in late medieval Marseille.* Ithaca, NY: Cornell University Press.

Smith, H. (2014). The thing about exclusion. *Brigham-Kanner Property Rights Conference Journal.* Harvard Law Working Paper No. 14–26.

Soja, E. (1989). *Postmodern geographies.* Brooklyn: Verso.

Squires, J. (1994). Private lives, secluded places: Privacy as political possibility. *Environment and Planning D: Society and Space, 12*(4), 387–401.

Standish, A. (1613). *New directions of experience authorized by the King's most excellent majesty, as may appear for the increasing of timber and firewood, with the least waste and loss of ground.*

Stanger-Ross, J. (Ed.). (2020). *Landscapes of injustice: A new perspective on the internment and dispossession of Japanese Canadians.* Montreal: McGill-Queens University Press.

Starblanket, G., & Hunt, D. (2018, February 13). How the death of Colten Boushie became recast as the story of a knight protecting his castle. *Globe and Mail.* https://news.umanitoba.ca/globe-and-mail-how-the-death-of-colten-boushie-became-recast-as-the-story-of-a-knight-protecting-his-castle/.

Suk, J. (2008). Taking the home. *Law and Literature, 20*(3), 291–317.

Suk, J. (2009). *At home in the law: How the domestic violence revolution is transforming privacy.* Yale University Press.

Sullivan, E. (2018). Dignity takings and "trailer trash": The case of mobile home park mass evictions. *Chicago-Kent Law Review, 92*(3), 937–959.

Sullivan, G. A. (1994). 'Arden lay murdered in that plot of ground': Surveying, land, and Arden of Faversham. *English Literary History, 61*(2), 231–352.

Sullivan, R. (1970, August 8). 2 Poverty aides seized at migrant's camp. *New York Times,* p. 19. www.nytimes.com/1970/08/08/archives/2-poverty-aides-seized-at-jersey-migrants-ca.

Sylvestre, M.-E., Blomley, N., & Bellot, C. (2020). *Red zones: Criminal law and the territorial regulation of marginalized people.* Cambridge: Cambridge University Press.

Taylor, E. G. R. (1947). The surveyor. *Economic History Review, 17*(2), 121–133.

Tennant, P. (1990). *Aboriginal peoples and politics.* Vancouver: University of British Columbia Territories. *Sociology, 49*(3), 438–454.

Thirsk, J. (1967). Farming techniques. In J. Thirsk (Ed.), *The Agrarian history of England and Wales, vol. IV* (pp. 161–199). Cambridge University Press.

Thirsk, J. (1983). Plough and pen: Agricultural writers in the seventeenth century. In T. H. Ashton, P. R. Coss, C. Dyer, & J. Thirsk (Eds.), *Social relations and ideas: Essays in honour of R.H. Hilton* (pp. 295–319). Cambridge: Cambridge University Press.

Thom, B. (2009). The paradox of boundaries in Coast Salish territories. *Cultural Geographies, 16*, 179–205.

Thompson, E. P. (1993). *Customs in common: Studies in traditional popular culture.* New York: The New Press.

Thompson, F. M. L. (1968). *Chartered surveyors: The growth of a profession.* London: Routledge, Kegan and Paul.

Thompson, R. (2007). Cultural models and shoreline social conflict. *Coastal Management, 35*(2), 211–237.

Tusser, T. (1873). *Five hundred pointes of good husbandrie.* London: Trubner and Company. (Original work published 1580)

Underkuffler, L. (2003). *The idea of property: Its meaning and power.* Oxford: Oxford University Press.

Van der Walt, A. J. (1999). Property rights and hierarchies of power: A critical evaluation of land reform policy in South Africa. *Koers, 64*(2/3), 259–294.

Van der Walt, A. J. (2009). *Property in the margins.* Oxford: Hart.

Vasudevan, A. (2015). The make-shift city: Towards a global geography of squatting. *Progress in Human Geography, 39*(3), 338–359.

Vasudevan, A. (2017). *The autonomous city: A history of squatting.* Brooklyn: Verso Books.

Walcott, R. (2021). *On property.* Biblioasis: Windsor.

Waldron, J. (1990). *The right to private property.* Oxford: Clarendon Press.

Waldron, J. (1991). Homelessness and the issue of freedom. *UCLA Law Review, 39*, 295–324.

Walter, J. (1985). A 'rising of the people'? The Oxfordshire rising of 1596. *Past and Present, 107*, 90–143.

Warren, S., & Brandeis, L. (1890). The right to privacy. *Harvard Law Review, 4*, 193.

Weisbord, N. (2018). Who's Afraid of the Lucky MOOSE? Canada's dangerous self-defence innovation. *McGill Law Journal/Revue de droit de McGill, 64*(2), 349–397.

Wolfe, P. (2006). Settler colonialism and the elimination of the native. *Journal of Genocide Research, 8*(4), 387–409.

Wolfe, P. (2016). *Traces of History: Elementary Structures of Race.* Verso, London.

Woodward, D., & Lewis, G. M. (1998). Introduction. In D. Woodward & F. M. Lewis (Eds.), *The history of cartography* (pp. 1–10, Vol. 2, Book 3). Chicago, IL: University of Chicago Press.

Worlidge, J. (1669). *Systema agriculturæ, being the mystery of husbandry discovered and layd open.* London.

Yeo, S. (2011). Killing a home invader. *Criminal Law Quarterly, 57*, 181–202.

Index

For Product Safety Concerns and Information please contact our EU
representative GPSR@taylorandfrancis.com
Taylor & Francis Verlag GmbH, Kaufingerstraße 24, 80331 München, Germany

www.ingramcontent.com/pod-product-compliance
Lightning Source LLC
Chambersburg PA
CBHW061332220326
41599CB00026B/5145